# TWAYNE'S WORLD AUTHORS SERIES

## A Survey of the World's Literature

Sylvia E. Bowman, Indiana University

**GENERAL EDITOR**

# FRANCE

Maxwell A. Smith, Guerry Professor of French, Emeritus
The University of Chattanooga
Former Visiting Professor in Modern Languages
The Florida State University

**EDITOR**

# Charles Nodier

*(TWAS 242)*

# TWAYNE'S WORLD AUTHORS SERIES (TWAS)

*The purpose of TWAS is to survey the major writers —novelists, dramatists, historians, poets, philosophers, and critics—of the nations of the world. Among the national literatures covered are those of Australia, Canada, China, Eastern Europe, France, Germany, Greece, India, Italy, Japan, Latin America, the Netherlands, New Zealand, Poland, Russia, Scandinavia, Spain, and the African nations, as well as Hebrew, Yiddish, and Latin Classical literatures. This survey is complemented by Twayne's United States Authors Series and English Authors Series.*

*The intent of each volume in these series is to present a critical-analytical study of the works of the writer; to include biographical and historical material that may be necessary for understanding, appreciation, and critical appraisal of the writer and to present all material in clear, concise English—but not to vitiate the scholarly content of the work by doing so.*

# Charles Nodier

### By HILDA NELSON
*San Diego State University*

Twayne Publishers, Inc.   ::   New York

To Burt

"Un seul être vous manque et tout est dépeuplé"

# *Preface*

Charles Nodier was an early pioneer of the Romantic movement, giving expression to *Wertherism* and the *mal du siècle* in
his works already in 1800, two years before the appearance of
*René*. Although Nodier's Romanticism, at least in its early stages,
was closely linked to the Monarchy, Catholicism, and Chivalry,
and concerned itself with giving France a national literature
steeped in the values and traditions of its past, he was also greatly
influenced by the literary trends that were making their way into
France from across the Channel and the Rhine. In addition to
Goethe's Werther, other elements such as the Outlaw of Schiller,
the many aspects of Byronism and vampirism, the gothic novel,
as well as the ideas of writers like E. T. A. Hoffmann, Achim von
Arnim, Tieck, Jean Paul—to name but a few—exerted, in varying
degrees and at various periods in his life, a marked influence
on his works. During the 1810s and the 1820s, after having evolved
through the cycle of *Wertherism*, Nodier, like so many others,
fell under the sway of the "genre frénétique," a form of Romanticism that expressed itself in such themes as the noble, generous
outlaw, and the demons of the night.

When, however, by 1830, Romanticism became more militant,
Nodier withdrew from the literary polemics of the age and devoted much of his time to the creation of a world of his own
making, a world in which he sought and found solace. This period
comprises the years between 1830 and 1844, and it marks the most
varied and the most creative period of his life. It is a period that
evinces, above all, a world which is steeped in the fantastic and
the marvelous, inhabited by the *voyants* and the innocents, but
where the shadow of anguish and fear incessantly lurks. This
period also reveals a Nodier playing the role of the "dériseur
sensé," that is, the judicious and critical mocker of society. Toward
the end of his life, Nodier sought more and more the world of pure

thought, which expressed itself in his mystical works and in which his interest in Illuminism, already apparent in his early youth, manifested itself even more markedly.

Nodier was one of the early contributors to the *conte fantastique* and can be considered as an important initiator in recording the impact of the dream, that is, the nocturnal dream which one experiences by night, as well as the diurnal dream, that state which approximates the dream when the individual creates a world of his own and when he is, as Poe put it, more "cognizant of many things which escape those who dream only by night."[1] It is, above all, the impact of the dream on the writer's psyche and its use in literary creation that is of paramount importance for Nodier. In this respect he antedates the Surrealists and anticipates Freud and Jung. It is also important to note that Nodier was equally aware of the evolution of the species, for his notion of palingenesis, although imbued with mysticism, also reveals that he believed in a branchlike theory of evolution. However, much of what Nodier has written has often been ignored by historians of literature who, in their manuals, merely refer to him as the bibliomane and librarian of the Arsenal who gathered together in his salon, between 1824 and 1828, all the great lions of Romanticism. It is only in recent years that Nodier is being given the attention he deserves.

When compared to such literary giants as Balzac, Stendhal, and Flaubert, Nodier lacks the intensity, the perseverance, and the literary robustness of these men; possibly he diverted his talents in too many directions. Nonetheless, even smaller names, genres, and currents in literature have their value and Nodier, unquestionably, influenced considerably the course of French literature, not only through his *contes fantastiques,* but also through his literary criticism which was always devoted to the defense of the new writers and the new movement.

HILDA NELSON

*San Diego State University* *
*San Diego, California*

* The Research for this book was supported in part by a grant from San Diego State University Foundation.

# *Contents*

# Contents

# Chronology

1780    29 April. Charles Nodier is born in Besançon, France, Mother is Suzanne Paris; father is unknown.

1791    Antoine-Melchior Nodier, lawyer, marries Suzanne Paris, his housekeeper, making his son legitimate—Charles Nodier is eleven years old. Charles gives a speech to the society of the *Amis de la Constitution* in Besançon. It is a patriotic speech and Charles is heralded as a child prodigy.

1792    Charles is made a member of the *Amis de la Constitution.*

1793    An old friend of the family, Justin Girod de Chantrans, teaches him botany, entomology, and mineralogy. Toward the end of the year he meets Euloge Schneider in Strasbourg who becomes his tutor.

1796    Nodier returns to Besançon and enrolls in the École Centrale. One of his professors is Victor Proud'hon. Together with Luczot de la Thébaudais, Nodier founds the secret society *Les Philadelphes.*

1798    With Luczot de la Thébaudais, Nodier publishes *Dissertation sur l'usage des antennes dans les insectes et sur l'organe de l'ouïe dans ces mêmes animaux.* Obtains a post as librarian.

1799    Nodier together with Weiss, Baud, and Monnot writes a parody making fun of the *Société populaire,* a Jacobin Club. Weiss and the others are arrested. Nodier escapes. He loses his post. Begins to edit the autobiography *Moi-même* that will be published in 1921.

1800    *Les Philadelphes* edit *Essais littéraires par une société de jeunes gens* in which Nodier publishes three poems. Nodier's first sojourn in Paris at the Hôtel de Hambourg in the rue de Grenelle-Saint-Honoré.

1801    Nodier returns to Besançon. Takes up again his post as librarian. September, presentation of a play written with

Francis at the Municipal Theatre of Besançon entitled *Lequel des deux ou l'Amant incognito*. Returns to Paris in October. Becomes member of *Les Méditateurs*, a secret society.

1802    Attends meeting of *Les Méditateurs* with Maurice Quaï, Joseph and Lucile Franque. Publishes *Stella ou les Proscrits*. Writes *La Napoléone*. Returns from Paris to Besançon.

1803    Second sojourn in Paris at the Hôtel de Berlin. *La Napoléone* is published in London. Publication of *Le dernier chapitre de mon roman*. Publication of *Le Peintre de Saltzbourg* and *Méditations du Cloître*. In December Nodier admits authorship of *La Napoléone*. He is arrested and imprisoned for thirty-six days.

1804    Publication of *Essais d'un jeune barde*. Nodier is under surveillance in Besançon.

1805    A conspiracy is discovered. Nodier escapes, errs about the countryside. He returns to Besançon and is placed in custody of his father.

1806    Publication of *Les Tristes ou Mélanges tirés des tablettes d'un suicide*.

1808    July. Thanks to Jean de Bry, Nodier begins his course in philosophy, literature, grammar, and natural history. August. Nodier marries Désirée-Liberté Charve, half-sister to Lucile Franque. 10 October. Death of Nodier's father. Publication of *Dictionnaire des onomatopées*. Plans to leave for Louisiana.

1809    2 January. Nodier continues his course at Dole. Jean de Bry proposes his membership to the Academy of Besançon.

1811    26 April. Birth of daughter Marie at Quintigny.

1812    12 March. Nodier becomes member of Academy of Besançon. Publication of *Questions de littérature légale* and *Museum entomologicum*. He obtains the post of librarian and director of *Le Télégraphe Illyrien* at Laybach (Ljubljana). December. The Nodier family are in Laybach.

1813    6 January. Nodier begins his new job. September. Nodier loses his post and returns to France. Collaborates with the *Journal de l'Empire*.

1814    The *Journal de l'Empire* becomes the *Journal des Débats*. Nodier continues to collaborate. Birth of Nodier's son Térence. Nodier is given the *Ordre du Lys* for loyalty to the House of Bourbon.

1815 Napoleon returns. The Hundred Days. Nodier publishes anonymously *Histoire des sociétés secrètes dans l'armée*. Napoleon disembarks at the Golf of Juan. Nodier seeks refuge.

1816 Death of his son Térence.

1818 Publication of *Jean Sbogar*. Nodier contemplates going into exile in Odessa where he is offered the chair of political science and the directorship of a newspaper. Waits in Quintigny for passports. The position does not materialize. He returns to Paris in October.

1819 Publication of *Thérèse Aubert*.

1820 Publication of *Adèle, Mélanges de littérature et de critque*. *Lord Ruthwen ou Les Vampires* by C. B. is published by the author of *Jean Sbogar* and *Thérèse Aubert*. 13 June. *Le Vampire* is presented at the Théâtre de la Porte Saint-Martin, written by Nodier in collaboration with Carmouche and Jouffroy. 25 August. Nodier is decorated with the Legion of Honor. He collaborates with the newspaper *Conservateur* and begins publication of *Voyages dans l'ancienne France* with Taylor and Cailleux.

1821 Birth of his son Amédée who dies a few months later. Publication of *Smarra*. 13 June. Nodier visits Scotland with Baron Taylor, Cailleux, and Isabey. Publication of *Promenade de Dieppe aux montagnes d'Ecosse*. Nodier, with Taylor, adapts Maturin's *Bertram or the Castle of Saint Aldobrand*. He begins to collaborate with *La Quotidienne*, a Royalist newspaper.

1822 Publication of *Essai sur la littérature romantique, Trilby ou le Lutin d'Argail, Infernaliana*, and *Essai sur la philosophie des langues, ou Théorie de l'Alphabet naturel*. Nodier writes a preface to an edition of *Thousand and One Nights*. In Volume I of the *Chefs-d'oeuvre des théâtres étrangers*, Nodier publishes an adaptation of *The Honey Moon of John Tobin*.

1823 Hugo, with collaboration of Soumet and Deschamps, founds *La Muse française*, a newspaper devoted to Romanticism, with which Nodier (*Tablettes romantiques*) collaborates. Nodier writes a review of Hugo's *Han d'Islande*.

Lamartine dedicates a poem from *Recueillements* to Nodier.

1824   3 January. Nodier is nominated librarian of the Count d'Artois at the Arsenal. Nodier publishes article on Hugo's *Nouvelles odes* in *La Quotidienne*.

1825   August. Nodier attends with Hugo, in an official capacity, the crowning of Charles X at Reims. He undertakes with the family Hugo a trip to Switzerland. They visit Lamartine.

1827   The friendship between Nodier and Hugo begins to cool off. He meets Sainte-Beuve.

1828   Publication of *Examen critique des Dictionnaires de la langue française*. Nodier's *Roi de Bohême* is in press.

1829   Publication of *Poésies* and *Mélanges tirés d'une petite bibliothèque*. Nodier sells his library to pay off his debts and to pay for his daughter's dowry. Nodier's article on Hugo's *Les Orientales* appears in *La Quotidienne*. Formation of *Le Cénacle*, a literary salon at the Hugos' which will give the death blow to the salon at l'Arsenal. Publication of *Souvenirs et Portraits de la Révolution Française*.

1830   Publication of *L'Histoire du Roi de Bohême et de ses sept châteaux*. 9 February. Marriage of Marie Nodier with Jules Mennessier. 22 July. Nodier loses his post as librarian. Publication of *Du Fantastique dans la littérature* and *Recherches sur le style*. Nodier is hurt in the leg. Publication of part of *Souvenirs de l'Empire*.

1831   Publication of *De quelques phénomènes du sommeil, M. de la Mettrie ou les Superstitions, De l'Amour et de son influence, comme sentiments sur la société actuelle*. Publishes in *La Revue de Paris* the *Mémoires of Maxime Odin*, published later as *Les Souvenirs de jeunesse*. Publication of *Le Bibliomane*. Loève-Weimars introduces him to *Le Temps*.

1832   Nodier tries twice to present himself to the French Academy, but without success. Publication of *L'Histoire d'Hélène Gillet, Jean-François les Bas-Bleus, Le Nouveau Faust et la nouvelle Marguerite* ( later called *L'Amour et le Grimoire* ), *Sibylle Mérian, Le Songe d'or, Mademoiselle de Marsan, De l'Utilité morale de l'instruction pour le peuple*. A cholera epidemic breaks out. Nodier sojourns for a while with his daughter and son-in-law in Metz. Publication of *De la Palingénésie humaine et de la résurrection* in

*La Revue de Paris.* Publication of *Lettre à Charles Nodier* by Balzac in *La Revue de Paris*. *La Fée aux miettes* appears for the first time as part of Volume IV of Nodier's *Oeuvres complètes*, published by Renduel.

1833 Publication of *Le Dernier banquet des Girondins, Baptiste Montauban, ou l'Idiot, La Combe de l'homme mort, Trésor des Fèves et Fleur des Pois, Hurlubleu, Leviathan-le-Long, Miscellanées.* 26 October. Nodier is received by the French Academy.

1834 Publication of *Notions de linguistique.* Nodier founds the *Bulletin du Bibliophile.*

1835 Publication of *Comment les patois furent détruits en France.*

1836 Publication of *Paul et la ressemblance, Voyage pittoresque et industriel dans le Paraguay-Roux, Piranèse, La Seine et ses bords, Monsieur Cazotte.*

1837 Publication of *Inès de la Sierras, Le Génie Bonhomme, La Légende de Soeur Béatrix.*

1838 Publication of *Les Quatre Talismans, La Neuvaine de la Chandeleur.*

1839 Publication of *Lydie ou la résurrection.*

1840 1 May. *Portrait littéraire* of Nodier by Sainte-Beuve appears in *La Revue des deux mondes.*

1841 Nodier writes a preface for an edition of the collected plays by his friend Guilbert de Pixérécourt.

1842 Publication of *Les Marionnettes.* Nodier is seriously ill.

1844 27 January. Death of Nodier at the Arsenal. Jules Janin publishes Nodier's *Franciscus Columna* posthumously.

# CHAPTER 1

# *Romanticism*

## I  *The Mal du Siècle, Its Nature and Causes*

A STUDY of the nineteenth century reveals a ferment and a multiplicity of ideas. It is an era which juxtaposes state absolutism and democracy, monarchy and republicanism, nationalism and cosmopolitanism, neomercantilism and *laissez-faire*. Extreme pessimism and cynicism coexisted with a facile optimism and a belief in progress, mysticism and occultism with positivism and skepticism, love for the multitudes with disdain for the masses, desire for communication and solidarity with estrangement and solitude. Philosophies rooted in experience and physical reality vied with rationalism and intuitionism and literary movements such as Romanticism, Art for Art's sake and Symbolism paralleled Realism and Naturalism. Indeed, all ages have had their contradictions, but at no time have these contradictions been as pronounced and as rich in diversity as they were in the nineteenth century. Frequently, some of these contradictions could be found within the same individual.

Set against this diverse background, witness the total demise of the *ancien régime*, which officially died in 1789, but which, in fact, lingered till the middle of the following century.[1] With the disintegration of the old order came the disintegration of such concepts as the divine right of kings, the honor of the gentleman and the traditional God.[2] A new revolution, the industrial revolution, whose preliminary phase had been ushered in between the years 1770 and 1830 in England, began to make itself felt in Continental Europe. It was primarily after the Napoleonic Wars that the main phase of this revolution began to make definite inroads on France with the introduction of machine production. After 1830 the French government began to be favorably disposed toward various industries, and faith in progress and social reform was intensified. The slogan which ushered in the bourgeois King

Louis-Philippe was: "Get rich through work." It must be noted that this is also the decade of important technological developments: introduction of gaslight, steam, and railroads. It was inventions or discoveries such as these that gave the impression that man was dominating nature and on the way to achieving the millennium.

The industrial revolution, with its introduction of mass production, the breaking up of the family, the rise of the proletariat, and the irresponsibility embedded in concepts of *laissez-faire* gave the old order the *coup de grâce*. With the loss of religion and the strong family unit, there arose a sense of rootlessness, a feeling of alienation which can only be compared with the alienation that was experienced after World War I and which, in part, gave rise to the Surrealist and Existentialist movements.

Romanticism was a revolt against much that was associated with the *ancien régime*. But it was also a revolt against the old literary strictures of the Classical period, a revolt against the strictures of reason and order, the classical unities, the separation of the tragic and the comic and the *moi haïssable*. Reduced to its essence, Romanticism was a reaction against rationalism and Classicism and stood for the expression of the emotions. In this sense, Romanticism was composed of a very loose group of writers who held similar basic ideals and ideas. The basic tone of their literature is one of anguish, dissatisfaction, and unrest. This literature turns its back on reality and, instead, extols the free play of the imagination and the dream. It grants to the domain of sentiment, inspiration, and individuality rights that had been condemned during the Classical period.

According to Paul Van Tieghem, there were two main events in the intellectual life of Europe: the Renaissance and Romanticism. Everything else that evolved was a mere extension of these two movements. Both caused severe disruptions in man's thinking and actions: both were revolts, severe breaks with the past, the one with the old scholastic thinking, the other with Classicism and rationalism. In both periods the intellectually aware underwent a severe crisis. In both eras man experienced estrangement, anguish, despair, and concerned himself with the human condition.

It has been noted earlier that Romanticism was a revolt against the old order. But Romanticism was also a revolt against the new order ushered in, to a large extent, by the industrial revolution.

Romanticists, especially those of the second generation, revolted
against the new men: the drab, money-grubbing, ambitious bourgeois, devoid of ideals and of culture, effectively portrayed in the
works of Balzac, Stendhal, and Flaubert. Charles Nodier, speaking for an earlier generation of Romanticists, expresses, in many
of his works, this disdain for the new era and the new man with
his new set of values. In the preface to *Les Quatre Talismans*
(1838), he says that greed and ambition "precipitate old nations
toward their ruin and are the only secret to our revolutions" [3] and
hopes that the worker will take cognizance of the fact that neither
riches, social position, nor the privileges of birth will make men
happy and free. Like so many of his contemporaries and succes-
sors, Nodier considered his era "an age when all the moral and
religious sentiments seem to have been exiled from earth." [4] To a
man like Nodier, the world could not be, as it had been in the
eighteenth century or as it was with the Romantic idealists such as
the Saint-Simoniens or Fourierists, a world in which mankind was
conceived as good, wise, just, rational, and on its way to attaining
the millennium. He could not hold such a concept because he had
seen revolutionary ideals turn into terrorism. He was never to forget the effectiveness of the guillotine; throughout his life he was
obsessed with severed, bloody heads and made numerous references to the revolution and its consequences. Like Nerval, Nodier
was never to forget that Jacques Cazotte was made a victim of the
revolution. In *Souvenirs de la Révolution,* where he makes his sentiments quite clear, Nodier explains: "As far as I'm concerned, I
have no other memories, and my disgust for the present, which has
only increased with the years, must have strengthened in me the
habit of living in the past." [5] Nerval, in a number of his works,
also shows repeated concern for the lost illusions of the young
during a later period. In *Sylvie,* his personal disenchantment is
juxtaposed with the disenchantment of an age:

We were then living in a strange period, such as usually succeeds
revolutions or the decline of great reigns. It was no longer the gallant
heroism of the Fronde, the elegant, dressed-up vice of the Regency, or
the scepticism and insane orgies of the Directoire. It was an age in
which activity, hesitation, and indolence were mixed up, together with
dazzling Utopias, philosophies, and religious aspirations, vague en-
thusiasms, mild ideas of a Renaissance, weariness with past struggles,
insecure optimisms—somewhat like the period of Peregrinus and

Apuleius. Material man longed for the bouquet of roses which would regenerate him from the hands of the divine Isis; the goddess in her eternal youth and purity appeared to us by night and made us ashamed of our wasted days. We had not reached the age of ambition, and the greedy scramble for honors and positions caused us to stay away from all posssible spheres of activity. The only refuge left to us was the poet's ivory tower, which we climbed, ever higher, to isolate ourselves from the mob. Led by our masters to those high places we breathed at last the pure air of solitude, we drank oblivion in the legendary golden cup, and we got drunk on poetry and love.[6]

In another work by Nerval, entitled *Aurélia,* the same lack of confidence, the same disillusionment with the age, is expressed after the July Revolution of 1830, when he speaks of "the years of scepticism and political and social depression that had followed the July Revolution. I had been one of the young men of that period and I had tasted its ardors and bitterness."[7]

Living in a period of instability, men such as Nodier, Nerval, Stendhal, Vigny, Musset (and to their names one could add many others) yearned for stability. Some, like Nerval, even yearned for religion, but were unable to believe in traditional religion because they were still a part of the eighteenth-century heritage, a heritage of skepticism or even indifference. They were in constant hesitation between a skepticism of which they were the unhappy victims through education, and a mysticism which they desired. It was, in part, this conflict, this duality, which agitated the age as well as the individual. When this quest for stability came to nought and the goal was not achieved, many tried to escape into a world of their own making. In their disillusionment, in their desire to escape from the world of reality, and in their attempt to discover solutions to their conflicts, men such as Nodier, Nerval, Musset, Gautier, and Baudelaire, often resorted to ways that were shortcuts, such as opium, hashish, and the like. But they also sought, and found, solace in the world of the imagination, the world of the dream. This feeling of *ennui,* anguish, and despair, this fear of the *néant,* the abyss, death, which accompanied their disillusionment and which is called the *mal du siècle* was a malady that gnawed at several generations.

It first appeared in Goethe's *Leiden des jungen Werthers,* in the *mal de René,* and in the cynicism of Byron. It manifested itself in an ardent imagination coupled with an attraction to strong sensa-

tions and a sense of *ennui*. All of its proponents experienced what
Chateaubriand called the *vague des passions*, which was, after all,
not much different from Pascal's anguish at experiencing the *mal
de l'infini* and the existential nausea that was prevalent among the
anguished of the post-World War II era. The young Werthers, the
Renés, the Byrons, ardent, pale, and nervous, tried to camouflage
their anguish in cynicism or in dandyism. The generation born or
growing up during the Napoleonic period was especially vulnerable. While reared to the bulletins of the *Grande Armée*, to the
sound of cannons, the beat of the drums, the *Te Deums*, to action,
they were suddenly, in 1815, condemned to inactivity and to living in a sort of limbo, a state between an old order, reintroduced
but doomed at the very outset because it had all the signs of tem-
porariness and lacked the definite values and disciplines of the
*ancien régime*, and a future that was dim and uncertain and
seemed never to come. This sense of lassitude, of frustration, this
*ennui* was felt even more when Louis-Philippe became king in
1830. In 1835, in *Servitude et Grandeur*, Vigny is speaking for his
generation as well as for the new one when he says:

> I belong to that generation born with the (nineteenth) century,
> which, fed upon the Emperor's bulletins, always had a drawn sword
> before its eyes, and which came to take it up at the very moment when
> France resheathed it in the Bourbon scabbard.[8]

Musset, a year later, expressed the same sense of malaise, the same
anguish and despair, in *La Confession d'un enfant du siècle:*

> A feeling of extreme uneasiness began to ferment in all young
> hearts. Condemned to inaction by the powers which governed the
> world, delivered to vulgar pedants of every kind, to idleness and to
> ennui, the youth saw the foaming billows which they had prepared to
> meet, subside. All these gladiators, glistening with oil, felt in the bot-
> tom of their souls an insupportable wretchedness. The richest became
> libertines; those of moderate fortune followed some profession and re-
> signed themselves to the sword or to the robe. The poorest gave them-
> selves up with cold enthusiasm to great thoughts, plunged into the
> frightful sea of aimless effort. . . .
> While life outside was so colorless and so mean, the interior life of
> society assumed a somber aspect of silence; hypocrisy ruled in all de-
> partments of conduct; . . .[9]

Indeed, when Chateaubriand presented his readers with the experience of the *vague des passions,* his intent was to condemn useless, sickly reveries and fantastic dreams. He wished to present an alternative to his malady, namely the simple Christian life and social virtues. Thus, when René says, "My sorrow had become an occupation which filled all my waking hours; so much had my heart molded itself to ennui and misery!," [10] he is actually condemning this condition. But, to the generations that read the works of Chateaubriand (and this included many generations), the *mal de René* became a source of imitation and inspiration rather than a condemnation.

Despite divergent ideas, despite divergent temperaments, likes and dislikes, one finds that a relatively large important group of writers was gripped by similar aspirations and frustrations, fears and despair, by the same sense of revolt against a world they had not made and over which they had no control. Many of these traits can be seen in the works of as diverse a group as Nodier, Vigny, Musset, Nerval, Flaubert, and Baudelaire. These individual manifestations may have been partly the result of the times, caused by the political, historical, and social milieu, partly the result of a personal temperament or disposition, an aberration or, perhaps, merely a pose. But, whatever the causes, the symptoms were there, namely, the terrible feeling of the *néant,* of nothingness, a metaphysical void. For behind all the anguish, the "fear and the trembling" (to use a Kierkegaardian term to express the same phenomenon), the *ennui,* lay the terrible paradox that men are mortal and that the universe is eternal. Because God and immortality were no longer concepts in which they could really believe and because values could no longer be considered permanent, a sense of certainty, of security, or peace of mind, was no longer possible. Thus several generations, like Pascal before them and the Existentialists after them, brooded over these feelings and frustrations and made desperate attempts to overcome them. Some, like Gautier, Baudelaire, Lautréamont, Rimbaud, and Laforgue, tried to overcome their fear of the *néant* by losing themselves in it, through the process of what is called *l'anéantissement,* a sort of merging with the universe, where the *I* becomes the *non-I,* where the *I* merges with objects. Many tried to escape the human condition as well as their personal fate through travel. Few traveled more avidly than did Romanticists such as Nodier,

Nerval, Gautier, Mérimée, Asselineau, and Flaubert. Their travels took them to Turkey, Egypt, Greece, as well as to Spain, Italy, Germany, and England. They traveled in search of new experiences, new sensations, and new images. They traveled eagerly to the Orient because, as Nerval said in his *Voyage en Orient,* the Orient was "the land of dreams and illusion." [11] Some traveled to escape their environments, sometimes to escape from themselves, to forget themselves. Nerval, for one, also traveled to discover secrets which could explain and cure his terrible malady, to search for a new self, to search for personal salvation.

But travel, as they soon came to realize, did not and could not afford them the means to escape. New lands, however exotic, are still composed of people—and people, no matter how superficially different and for all the local color, show surprisingly identical traits with those one has just left behind. It was, after all, still the real world with which they came in contact, the world with its boundaries and limitations of space and time. Thus, an interest in the occult and in Oriental mysticism was developed in the belief that the supernatural and the mystical would afford them this escape. Mesmerism, galvanism, Free Masonry, and the cult of the Goddess Isis began to find adherents among the Romanticists. Numerology, metempsychosis, metapsychosis, palingenesis, mostly of Oriental origin, also found strong support. Lavater and Swedenborg, with their concepts of correspondences and analogies, influenced such men as Nodier, Nerval, Gautier, and Baudelaire. Terms such as *une vie antérieure* and *déjà vu* began to find their way into literature. Interest in the Illuminists and in such men as Restif de la Bretonne and Jacques Cazotte grew, for in them were detected kindred spirits; in them they could discern a keen interest in the world of the imagination, the dream, as well as in the occult. Interest in the occult was, of course, nothing new. The Middle Ages, even the Renaissance and the seventeenth century, evinced an interest in it. Man has always wanted to know, and since knowledge of the physical world, of reality, seemed limited, the occult, it was felt, might permit man to go beyond the world of appearances and enable him to overcome the limitations of the mind and the strictures of knowledge. The Romanticists, too, longed to overcome the last barrier, that eternal enigma: the nature of death and of life after death. They desired to experience all, even death; thus, the fear of and fascination with the *néant.*

They were in search of a *frisson nouveau*. Any path leading to it was worthy of investigation. Baudelaire, in *Les Fleurs du mal*, concludes his poem *Le Voyage* with the following lines: "To plunge to the bottom of the gulf, Hell or Heaven, what matter? To the bottom of the Unknown to find something *new*." [12]

Those with genius were quick to realize that there were more lasting and gratifying ways of escape as well as of opening the doors of perception. Baudelaire, for one, although he tried all the available methods of escape, including drugs, came to the realization that the *paradis artificiels* achieved through drugs were only in direct proportion to one's creative talent, capable of bringing forth only that which was already within one. Along with other Romanticists such as Nodier, Gautier, and Nerval, Baudelaire believed that the imagination, that "reine des facultés," was the only source of artistic creation, and thus the only effective and lasting means of escape. By means of the imagination the artist could create a world of his own making, a world over which he had complete control. Through the creative adventure of the mind, the artist could have visions that were boundless and unlimited. Even when he expressed his despair and his nightmares as well as his aspirations and dreams in the very world he was creating, he was able to rise above them; he was able to rise above reality and life with its banalities, its frustrations, its pettiness, greed, lust, and dishonesty. He could, in short, become god and, like God, be aloof and objective, "paring his fingernails."

## II   *The Nature of the Dream*

Charles Asselineau, friend of Baudelaire and co-editor of the posthumous edition of his collected works, entitled his own volume of short stories *La Double Vie*, referring thereby to the dichotomy between reality and experience on the one hand, and imagination, the world of the dream, the creative adventure, on the other. It is not without reason that Asselineau chose this title for his work, for it expressed an idea that was prevalent among his own generation, those immediately preceding and those succeeding it, in France as well as in England, Germany, Italy, and Russia.[13]

To analyze the nature of this dichotomy, that is the nature of the real and the imaginary world, as well as to give it artistic expression, has been man's concern since the Greeks. To understand the nature of the universe and man's place in that universe;

to go beyond the world of appearances, the superficial reality, with its limitations of time and space; to discover another reality that might reveal an answer to the enigma; to explore the theory of knowledge, with the question of whether the physical world exists or whether it is the figment of man's imagination, has been the concern of such great thinkers as Plato, Descartes, Berkeley, Hume, Kant, and many others.

It has been noted earlier that Romanticism was a reaction against such important concepts as rationalism, Classicism, or Neoclassicism, nature and natural law; concepts that had, to a very large degree, become deified during the age of Enlightenment in France by the *Philosophes,* the *Idéologues,* and the *Physiocrates.* Generally speaking, man, in the eighteenth century, believed that the exterior world was a real world and that his senses produced an exact copy of this world. Carl Becker, in *The Heavenly City of the 18th Century Philosophers,* discusses the underlying preconceptions of the age and tries to show that the *Philosophes* were victims of common sense, rationalism, natural law, and the like, and that they rationalized much in the name of these concepts. Of the *Physiocrates,* Becker says: "Search the writings of the new economists and you will find them demanding the abolition of artificial restrictions on trade and industry in order that men may be free to follow the natural law of self-interest." [14] This is, however, not to say that the ideas of the Enlightenment did not find adherents at various periods of the nineteenth century—we have only to remember the Fourierists, the Saint-Simoniens, the positivists; nor is it to say that the reaction against rationalism and Classicism did not find expression already during the eighteenth century in Restif de la Bretonne, Jacques Cazotte, Rousseau, and Diderot. One has only to remember Diderot's statement: "Poetry demands something that is gigantic, barbarous, and savage."

The idea of denying reason its unchallenged position on a pedestal was already very much in the air by the end of the eighteenth century. In Germany, Kant, in his *Critique of Pure Reason* (1781), had already begun to undermine the excesses of the rationalists of the eighteenth century and to set limits to the range of the human intellect. While challenging the rationalists, Kant also challenged man's notions of understanding reality as a thing in itself; reality could only be comprehended through the senses, that is, subjectively. The idea of denying phenomena an existence independent of man's perception of it was soon to find expression in the writings of other men, such as Hegel, Novalis, Schelling, Fichte, the Schlegel brothers, and Herder. Fichte, Kant's disciple, not only accepted the limitations of human reason but developed the idea that man's imagination was limitless and all-powerful.

This preoccupation with the nature of reality, and the imagination and the dream has not been the exclusive property of philosophers, scientists, or theologians. Poets, painters, writers, whether they call themselves Classicists, Romanticists, Realists, Naturalists, Symbolists, or Surrealists, have all, explicitly or implicitly, tried to come to grips with many of these problems. All have, to varying degrees, been curious about the nature of this dichotomy and have opted for one side in preference to the other. They have gone in search of knowledge, and many have tried to go beyond the world of appearances in search of this knowledge. Many have felt that it exists in the world of the imagination—the dream.

Reality is generally considered to be the routine, the prosaic, the given, that which one experiences. It expresses itself in the mere recording of childhood experiences; it expresses itself in the straightforward travel account. It finds its roots in the banalities of life, in the actual—actual settings, actual events—unchanged and objective. It is found in documents, in the recording of data. It is direct experience that is uncontaminated by the creative faculty. It is, as Albert Béguin puts it, that which is *autrui, objective,* "hors de nous." [15] It is, to a large extent, what science is about. But, one wonders, does this unchanged and objective recording of data really exist? Man is, after all, the measure of all things and the physical world, reality, can be experienced (as Kant and the Phenomenologists say) only in terms of man, that is, subjectively. Particularly in science, man must make use of his imagination to create the intellectual structures so essential to theory. Thus one may wonder whether, practically speaking, objective, "pure" reality actually exists.

It has by now become a truism to say that the imagination is an essential element in the creative adventure; and that without it there can be no art. The task of the artist is to take the given, that is, his experience of reality, to assimilate this experience and, with the aid of his own inner consciousness and genius, refashion this world of sensory experience to his own purpose, to his own vision of life. In other words, art must try to integrate, consolidate, interpret, and illuminate experience acquired through the senses, and thereby give meaning and form to what was heretofore meaningless and in a state of chaos. Thus, to cite Nietzsche, art is not an imitation of nature, but "a metaphysical supplement" [16] to the reality of nature.

Defining this dichotomy in these terms would seem to imply that the elements which go to make up the two worlds, namely, the world of physical reality and the world of the imagination, the dream, are one and the same and that the difference that exists is merely one of degree rather than one of kind; that the process which the mind undergoes is the same whether it is recording facts, that is, physical reality, or whether it is creating an imaginary world. What is different in kind is the ability to rearrange, to interpret, to give this reality one's own imprint, one's own meaning. "Be it as it may," says Nerval, "I believe that man's imagination has invented nothing that is not real, be it in this world or in others." [17]

Goethe was one of the first poets to consider the problem of the *double vie* dramatically and poetically. The problem of the world of reality and the world of the dream is poignantly expressed through Faust:

> Two souls, alas, are housed within my breast,
> And each will wrestle for the mastery there.
> The one has passion's craving crude for love,
> And hugs a world where sweet the senses rage;
> The other longs for pastures fair above,
> Leaving the murk for lofty heritage.
> O spirits, if there be, that range the air,
> Swaying in potency 'twixt heaven and earth,
> Come down, from out your golden skyey lair,
> Bear me to beauteous life, another birth.[18]

Like Faust before them, men such as Nodier, Nerval, Gautier, Baudelaire, Asselineau, to name but a few, tried to solve the conflict that this dichotomy imposes upon them. With little or no exception, these writers stress the dream, for it is precisely this world, the world of the imagination, that "reine des facultés," that produces the creative adventure. Nodier, for example, repeatedly states that he abhors reality, especially in art: "I have often expressed the idea that I hated the real in art, and my impression is that I have scarcely changed my mind." [19] Later it is true, in an introductory statement to *L'Histoire d'Hélène Gillet,* he says that he prefers the *fantastique vrai,* but he is using the term to indicate his dislike for the *fantastique* that deals exclusively with non-human elements, with ghosts, vampires, and the like. Baudelaire became increasingly convinced that *la vie intérieure* was immeasurably better than *la vie extérieure.* In *Les Projets* he says: "I have possessed three homes . . . and was actually happy in all of them. Why should I drive my body from place to place, when my soul travels so lightly? And why carry out one's projects, since the project is sufficient pleasure in itself?" [20] This "negative" attitude toward the real, the physically experienced, is a typical Romantic trait: anticipation of an event, a project, a voyage, or being with one's beloved, is more pleasurable than the actual experience. The imagination is thus more powerful, more "real" than reality, for only in anticipation is the imagination functioning. Nerval took a similar attitude with respect to the superiority of the imagination over physical reality. In his *Voyage en Orient* he admires a Mont Blanc of his own creation, a Mont Blanc "in the form of an immense white and red cloud, made tangible by the dream of my imagination . . . as to the real Mont Blanc, you can well understand that it made little impression on me." [21] In a letter to Jules Janin dated 16 November 1843 Nerval is even more emphatic about the superiority of the world of imagination, the dream over the world of reality: "In short, the Orient does not come close to this type of waking dream that I had two years ago, or else it is because that Orient is either too far or too high to reach, and I have had enough of running after poetry; I believe that it is at your door-step or perhaps in your bed." [22]

Escape into the world of the dream, that is the dream as the equivalent of another life—not necessarily experienced during sleep—a world of the active imagination, a world of evasion and solace, is not the only aspect that is pertinent to this discussion. Relevant also is the dream as defined as that which one experiences during sleep, which is composed of images and symbols and which is a way of expressing suppressed desires and emotions and, like the dream that is cognizant, can also be a menacing world, full of anguish, terror, and despair. According to Béguin, the dream is that which is *personnel, subjectif,* and "en nous." [23] It is composed of elements of reality, experience, retained by memory or the unconscious and conjured up at a given time. Through the dream, it is felt, man can penetrate into the innermost and secret parts of the mind, the subconscious, and thereby gain insight leading to the discovery of the self and the universe, a universe that is intangible and beyond the world of appearances. The dream also has prophetic properties and is a source of and means to knowledge, the kind of knowledge that is valuable and lasting.

The use of the dream in its more limited sense is, of course, nothing new. Dreams have played an important role in the Bible as well as in Greek and Roman mythology. The descent of Ulysses into hell is, as Nodier says, but a long, extended dream.[24] In the *Iliad*, gods and goddesses appear to the warriors in dreams and visions, urging them, cautioning them, coaxing, threatening, and praising them. In the *Golden Ass* by Lucius Apuleius, a work that will serve as model for the bizarre dream in Nodier's *La Fée aux miettes*, the dream is a strange phenomenon, full of ill omen. Dreams have prophetic qualities in *La Chanson de Roland*, as well as in many dramas of the sixteenth and seventeenth centuries. In the eighteenth century, for example, dreams are evident in such works as Diderot's *Les Bijoux indiscrets* and Jacques Cazotte's *Le Diable amoureux;* they also play an important role in the gothic novels. But it is largely with the Romanticists, especially the German Romanticists, that the dream begins to play such a significant role in literature as well as in the psychic life of man. French Romanticists, especially those familiar with and influenced by the works of the German Romanticists, were also cognizant of the importance of the nocturnal dream. Nerval, for one, was well aware of the impact of the dream on life and its use in art. Almost all of his works contain at least one dream episode. Referring to this secret world of the dream, Nerval says in *Aurélia*:

Our dreams are a second life. I have never been able to penetrate without a shudder those ivory or horned gates which separate us from the invisible world. The first moments of sleep are an image of death; a hazy torpor grips our thoughts and it becomes impossible for us to determine the exact instant when the "I," under another form, continues the task of existence. Little by little a vague underground cavern grows lighter and the pale gravely immobile shapes that live in limbo detach

themselves from the shadows and the night. Then the picture takes
form, a new brightness illumines these strange apparitions and gives
them movement. The spirit world opens before us.[25]

Charles Asselineau, in one of his *contes*, makes a perceptive observation with respect to the phenomenon of the dream:

What I find rather surprising in the life of the dream, is not so much
the fact that one finds oneself transported into regions that are fantastic
and in which all the habits one has acquired and the ideas one has received are confused and contradicted, and where (which is even more
frightening) the impossible mingles with the real. What is even more
striking is the ease with which we accept these contradictions and
monstrous fallacies as though they were something quite natural, and
in such a way that one can almost believe in faculties or notions that
are peculiar and foreign to our world.[26]

## III   *The* Conte Fantastique, *Its Nature and Origins*

Nowhere is the power of the imagination, that is, the use of the
dream during sleep and its impact on the psychic life of man and
the problem of the *double vie* more pronounced than in the *conte
fantastique*. Nowhere is the attempt to create another world, a
world with its own time and space, more fully developed than in
works such as *La Fée aux miettes, Trilby, ou le Lutin d'Argail,*
and *Smarra* by Nodier, or in the works of Nerval, works such as
*Sylvie, Aurélia,* and his oriental tales *Histoire du Caliphe Hakem*
and *Histoire de la Reine du matin et de Soliman Prince des
génies,* both part of *Voyage en Orient.* These same elements are
also prominent in Gautier's *Contes fantastiques,* as well as in his
*nouvelles, Spirite* and *Le Roman de la momie.* They are equally
apparent in Mérimée's *La Vision de Charles IX* and *Djoûmane,*
Villiers de l'Isle-Adam's *Véra,* and Barbey d'Aurevilly's *Les Dia-
boliques.* The imaginative quality and, more specifically, the
dreamlike quality, is very dominant in the *conte fantastique.* In
them the creation of the *double vie,* a life of illusion and the re-
production of the nightmarish qualities of life and the dream, is to
be found in its most obvious forms. It is in these works that the
imagination, under the guise of reality, reigns supreme; it is in
them that the attempt is made to get beyond the physical reality
and enter the unknown realms where space and time are eliminated, where nothing but the mind exists. This flight into the

world of the imagination, the *vie intérieure*, the dream, is not necessarily a pleasant one; it is often a cruel and brutal intrusion on
one's psychic life, often expressing the morbid states of one's unconscious. In these works an attempt is made to explore the inner
space of the mind, bringing to the surface dreams, visions, delir-
iums, and nightmares. These expressions of the inner mind are all
projected against a background that is familiar, namely physical
reality, which is, after all, the only background actually known.
Marcel Schneider in *La Littérature fantastique en France* says
that "the fantastic is the real which one must look at with other
eyes; it is also an inner space," [27] which are precisely those qualities found in the dream.

The dream or the approximation of the dream made concrete in
a *conte fantastique* has been used in many ways by various writers. In Nodier's *Smarra*, which will be discussed later, Nodier has
tried to present an actual dream as narrated by the dreamer, with
all the digressions and inconsistencies, the fears and anxieties and
morbid states of mind that real dreams entail. Gautier in some of
his *contes fantastiques* such as *La Cafetière* and *Le Club des
Hachichins* also tried to portray an experience as it is dreamed
naturally or under the influence of hashish. Secondly, there is the
insertion of a dream sequence within a larger work, such as the
descent of the sculptor Adoniram into the bowels of the earth in
Nerval's *Histoire de la Reine du matin et de Soliman Prince des
génies*, or the dreams the narrator has in *Aurélia* and *Pandora*.
Dream sequences also occur in Nodier's major work *La Fée aux
miettes*. A third use of the dream can be seen in the idea of a
*double vie*, a theme very much apparent in Gautier's *La Morte
amoureuse*, and Nodier's *Lydie ou la Résurrection*. In these *contes
fantastiques*, as in many others, the line of demarcation between
the world of physical reality and the world of the dream, that is,
the diurnal dream, has almost, if not completely, disappeared.
The characters move freely from one world into another.

The *conte fantastique* often gives the impression that it is built
upon a dream, that it is composed unconsciously, as if the narrator, be he outside the tale or part of it, were writing in a trance. In
their violations of the rules of reality, one can say that the creators
of the fantastic are in revolt against the human condition, that
they feel the need to reshape human destiny and thus create works
with their own rules of logic and laws of nature. In these works,

these writers, like so many of their characters, express a revolt which began with Lucifer and Prometheus and which is also visible in Cain, Don Juan, and Faust. For it is to combat the human condition and to conquer his fate that man has been compelled to have dreams and to create myths (collective dreams). Prometheus, a young god, defied older and more powerful gods to help mankind and for this he was punished.

The *conte fantastique* is permeated with an atmosphere of fatality and revolt, often acquiring an undertone of the satanic, satanism being itself an act of revolt. Often these works are instilled with a sense of the grotesque or the burlesque, a quality that André Breton calls *l'humour noir* and Baudelaire calls *le comique absolu* in his essay *De l'Essence du rire*. Furthermore, the creation of these works has served as a refuge from the many deceptions and the lost illusions forced upon the writers by a crude and alien world. "And," says Baudelaire, "the more ambitious and delicate the soul, all the more impossible the dreams. Every man possesses his own dose of natural opium, ceaselessly secreted and renewed." [28] Writers such as Nodier, Gautier, Villiers de l'Isle-Adam, and Mérimée, chose the form of the *conte fantastique* or the *nouvelle fantastique* because it allowed them to express themselves with considerable freedom, since they were dealing with a world of their own creation, a world with its own time, space, and logic; but they were always mindful of the fact that they were stressing the human element, man's inner psyche. The writer of the *conte fantastique* could express his anguish, his terrors, and his suppressed desires just as he could and did express them in a dream. He could be as creative as he wished as long as there was consistency within the fabric of his work. Just as the writers revolted against the human condition and escaped into a world of the imagination, the dream, so did their characters seek a world of the dream in an attempt to revolt against the human condition.

The fantastic with its stress on the *fantastique intérieur* became exceedingly popular in France around 1830. Before 1830 much of the *fantastique* can be characterized as being primarily *extérieur* or *frénétique*, having taken its cue from the gothic tales and stressing such elements as vampires, ghosts, and the like. Nodier's early works contain some of these elements. *Le Vampire*, written in collaboration with Carmouche and Jouffroy, and *Smarra* are two such examples. Nodier's most productive period took place

during the 1830's. The same can be said for Gautier who wrote
most of his *contes fantastiques* in the 1830's. Essays on the fantastic and the marvelous were filling reviews and newspapers, and
the *Revue de Paris* became the mouthpiece for the fantastic as
well as for E. T. A. Hoffmann. The essay that was of particular
importance in bringing both the fantastic and Hoffmann (if nega-
tively) to the attention of the French public was the one by
Walter Scott entitled *On the Supernatural in Fictitious Composition* which appeared in the *Revue de Paris* in 1829. (This essay
had originally appeared in the *Foreign Quarterly Review* in
1827.) In it Scott condemned the overuse of the *fantastique
extérieur* and said that the marvelous must not occur too often
and must keep a certain distance, for familiarity breeds contempt.
However, despite his condemnation of the use of ghosts, mon-
sters, giants, genii, fairies, and the like, Scott's essay reveals that
he did not regard the fantastic quite in the same light as it was
understood by French writers around 1830. To him, the fantastic
or marvelous had to exclude such elements as the grotesque or the
burlesque. Thus he condemned

the FANTASTIC mode of writing,—in which the most wild and unbounded licence is given to an irregular fancy, and all species of combination, however ludicrous, or however shocking, are attempted and
executed without scruple. In the other modes of treating the supernatural, even that mystic region is subjected to some laws, however
slight; and fancy, in wandering through it, is regulated by some prob-
abilities in the wildest flight. Not so in the fantastic style of composition, which has no restraint save that which it may ultimately find in
the exhausted imagination of the author.[29]

Shortly after the appearance of this essay in the *Revue de Paris,*
the publisher Renduel asked Scott to write the preface to an illus-
trated edition of Hoffmann's tales, entitled *Contes fantastiques.*
According to Castex, "Walter Scott, far from changing his opinion, placed the last paragraph of his article on the Supernatural at
the head of this preface (which, by the way, had provoked some
sharp retorts), and then proceeded to attack the German teller of
tales." [30] Scott not only attacked Hoffmann for what he considered his extravagances, his vagabond life, his unhealthy pessimism
and his madness; what is more important, he attacked Hoffmann
for his lack of poetic qualities. Scott's condemnation of this aspect

of the fantastic, namely, the grotesque or the burlesque, and especially the condemnation of Hoffmann and the German Romanticists, released a veritable deluge of articles in defense of both the
fantastic and of Hoffmann.

The influence of Hoffmann on European and American literature was enormous. Interest in Hoffmann occurred in France
around 1822 when Dr. Koreff, an intimate friend of Hoffmann,
settled down in Paris shortly after the author's death. He immediately became very much in demand in French literary circles. It
was Koreff who had initiated Hoffmann into the occult and had
introduced him to such ideas as metempsychosis, metapsychosis,
palingenesis, mesmerism, magnetism, and the like. It was undoubtedly Koreff whom Gautier had in mind in his portrayal of
the doctor in the *nouvelle Avatar*. Initially four names are closely
linked with the dissemination of information on Hoffmann's life
and works and with bringing him to the attention of the French
public. Besides Dr. Koreff, the three other names involved are
Loève-Veimars, Hoffmann's first French translator, Jean-Jacques
Ampère and Saint-Marc Girardin, his first French critics. One
after the other, they came to the defense of Hoffmann. In this battle between Scott and Hoffmann, it was the former who was the
loser; his reputation, already on the wane, was irremediably damaged. In 1830 Nodier published an article in the *Revue de Paris*
entitled *Du Fantastique dans la littérature* in which he traces elements of the fantastic from Homer to the German Romanticists
and considers the fantastic one of the most important elements in
the literature of the imagination. Nodier shows a particular affinity
for the German Romanticists, in general, and for Hoffmann, in
particular. In an essay aso written in 1830, Sainte-Beuve says:

Hoffmann then came and discovered on the edges of the real and visible universe, some dark, mysterious and, heretofore, unknown corner
and taught us to discern the special reflections, the strange shadows,
and the intricate machinery between that area and the earth, giving us
a whole new unforeseen mirror image of the natural perspectives and
human destinies familiar to us.[31]

The 1830's do, indeed, suggest a beginning of the polarization
of art, a polarization between two esthetic principles: art as a
means of expressing ideas and serving as a tribune for the people,

on the one hand, and art for art's sake, on the other. However, the writings of such men as Nodier, Nerval, Gautier (at least the Gautier of the *Contes fantastiques*), Baudelaire, Asselineau, and Stendhal, reveal, fortunately, a synthesis of the two concepts. Art is neither the crude expression of utilitarianism or propaganda; neither is it exclusively art for art's sake which, aside from expressing form rather than content, also leaves out man. Rather, art is a means of exploring that invisible universe; it is an attempt to lift man above himself, above his world of physical reality. Art is the product of the poet's vision of the world, his world and his truth.

# CHAPTER 2

# *The Wertherian Cycle*

## I  *The Alter Ego*

MUCH of the work of Nodier can be divided artificially into two parts: one part contains his creative works, the works of the imagination, the creative adventure of the mind; the other contains his numerous essays, articles, historical portraits, memoirs and travel accounts. Some of his works are autobiographical or semi-autobiographical and it is, indeed, often difficult to decide whether to place them with his creative works or to introduce a third category in which to place them. To make matters more complicated, Nodier has projected himself in his fiction both as narrator and as author under numerous names. Many of his autobiographical works have appeared under the name of Maxime Odin; but Maxime Odin also appears as the author of some of his tales. In an early autobiographical work he has also called himself Charles-Anonyme Trois-Étoiles.

Like all artists since time immemorial, Nodier had the desire and the need to be another self and thus conjured up a secret life or lives with a secret self or selves. The need to set up for oneself many parallel lives with a set of names to fit the occasion has afflicted writers such as Stendhal, Nerval, Boris Vian, to name but a few. More importantly, all writers project a part of themselves in their works. Or, as Proust put it in *Contre Sainte-Beuve*, "a book is the product of a different *self* from the self we manifest in our habits, in our social life, in our vices. If we would try to understand that particular self, it is by searching our own bosoms, and trying to reconstruct it there, that we may arrive at it." [1] Flaubert, when he allegedly exclaimed "Madame Bovary, c'est moi," was presumably referring to that "cancer of lyricism" that was gnawing within him and which he was trying to suppress. It was, in a sense, his other self.

The problem of the literary lie, the creative dream or reverie, is a common one in literature. Both Goethe and Rousseau, for example, made ample use of it. Goethe was perhaps more honest in that he called his semi-autobiography *Dichtung und Wahrheit,* the "Dichtung" having a double meaning: fabrication and poetizing or creating; "Wahrheit" meaning truth, reality. Rousseau, by calling his work *Confessions,* left himself more vulnerable to criticism. Nevertheless, one can say that the literary lie or creative lie is as valid in literature as is the presentation of "real" events. As has already been pointed out, the imagination, the dream, was as real, if not more real, to such writers as Goethe, Stendhal, Nodier, Nerval, and others, as was the notion of reality. To try to get at the event "the way it happened" is perhaps interesting but does not lend itself to any greater appreciation of the work. There is no doubt that the works of Goethe and Rousseau, as those of Nodier and Nerval, gained through their use of the literary lie. Furthermore, the lie, or suppressed information, is often more revealing of the author than what he has truthfully and diligently recorded. Indeed, letters, journals, and the like, although they may give clues, are often dubious corroborations, since in letters, for example, one often tries to present a "touched-up" portrait for the benefit of the recipient or even for posterity.

In many ways, Nodier's childhood is the story of many Romanticists. In his teens he was a nervous, shy, and hypersensitive youth, suffering from the fact that he was an illegitimate child, the son of a servant girl, whom his father eventually married when Charles was eleven years of age. To overcome his many pressing afflictions and weaknesses, Nodier needed an other self, an alter ego, an opposing but complementary self. Being excessively timid in the presence of women, it is understandable that he would often try to present himself as a Don Juan or a Valmont, an imaginative and resourceful seducer and lover. Thus, in his fertile and febrile imagination, Nodier was forever seducing older women when young, and young girls when older, although more in his imagination than in reality. Thus, throughout his works, but especially in his early *contes* and *nouvelles,* we discern a Nodier as he projects himself in his fiction, an anguished and suffering hero named Charles, Gaston, or Albert, loving and being loved, but whose love is never fulfilled and who either has to die, a victim of the whims of fate, or who sees his beloved die, equally a victim of fate. In his second preface to *Thérèse Aubert,* he says that "I can justify myself for having written so many useless novels only by repeating over and over again that they, like my prefaces, are a kind of novel of my own life." [2] But we also discover a rather different Nodier in the guise of Maxime Odin or Charles-Anonyme Trois-Etoiles. In *Moi-même*, an autobiographical pastiche, written around 1800 but published as late as 1921, Nodier portrays himself as a libertine to compensate for Nodier, the timid and anguished youth. He himself alludes to this propensity to lead parallel lives when he says in *Moi-même*: "My character is composed of heterogeneous elements and I am unable to resemble myself for ten consecutive minutes." [3] (He has read his Montaigne very diligently, it seems.) In *Le Dernier Chapître de mon roman* (1803), a sequel to *Moi-même*, the tone is very reminiscent of eighteenth-century libertine tales, and names such as Diderot and *Les Bijoux indiscrets*, Laclos and *Les Liaisons dangereuses*, Laurence Sterne and his *Sentimental Journey* and *Tristam Shandy* come to mind. Later, in 1831, in his *Souvenirs de jeunesse*, published under the name of Maxime Odin and which is a collection of portraits of young girls, we see the author/narrator occasionally playing the role of seducer and lover; this is especially true of the tale entitled *Lucrèce et Jeanette*, which constitutes the last story in this collection. In another work, *L'Amour et le grimoire ou le nouveau Faust* (1832), the hero is portrayed as a libertine by avocation and virtue is treated in a mock-serious tone.

Although Nodier's extreme nervous condition, his excessive exaltation, which alternated with his excessive timidity and melancholia, his extremely fertile imagination contributed extensively to his frame of mind and temperament, much of his feeling of *malaise* and *ennui* can be attributed to the malady that was afflicting whole generations of young men. Two works that contributed to this feeling of *malaise* and which were, themselves, manifestations of this "grand mal dans la morale," [4] were Rousseau's *Julie ou la nouvelle Héloïse* (1761) and Goethe's *Die Leiden des jungen Werthers* (1774). These two works were to set the tone in literature as well as in the life style of the young of several generations. Thus with Nodier, as with many other Romanticists, the sense of *ennui*, despair, anguish—traits that belonged to many generations of young men who felt that the world was out of joint —was a personal as well as a cultural phenomenon. Man, Nodier

felt, with his mania for progress and perfectibility, had lost his
innocence and society had become essentially evil and corrupt.
Thus, escape into the world of the imagination, the dream, as well
as an other self, was a refuge from an alien and menacing universe. In the world of his own making, Nodier was able to find
solace that was definite and positive. Nodier, unlike Nerval, was
successful in this attempt because he managed to maintain a
proper balance; he was able, as Nerval was not, to synthesize the
*double vie;* that is, he was able to bring together two parts of his
personality: the man who lived in the real world, the man of action, the *savant,* the academician and bibliophile; and the man of
dreams, the man who possessed a fertile imagination. He had, as
Jung put it, a "point of support" with this world: his books, his
friends, his family. What Jung says with respect to his own life is
surely applicable to Nodier: "It was most essential for me to have
a normal life in the real world as a counterpoise to that strange
inner world . . . assuring me that I was an actually existing ordinary person. The unconscious contents could have driven me
out of my wits." [5]

## II  *The Early Works*

The early works of Nodier, those that belong to what Castex
calls the Wertherian cycle, have, without exception, been affected
by Goethe's *Werther.* All his heroes, the Gastons, the Charles, the
Alberts, and, for that matter, even Maxime Odin, are prototypes
of Werther. They love passionately, uncompromisingly and see
death and suicide as the only way out of their afflictions and di-
lemmas. Already in a letter written in 1800, Nodier expressed very
succinctly and dramatically (perhaps even melodramatically), his
sense of anguish, despair, and *ennui:* "At twenty, I had seen everything, known everything, forgotten everything. At twenty, I
drained the cup of all sorrows, and, after having become involved
with useless hopes, I became aware, at twenty, that happiness was
not made for me." [6] This is the man of destiny, *l'homme fatal,*
whose path has been mapped out for him and from which there is
no digression and deliverance. These words express the sensibility
and the despair of the hypersensitive young men of the age, a
sensibility and, perhaps, a pose, that will be portrayed over and
over again in many of the works of Nodier. For Nodier, even perhaps more so than Chateaubriand or Senancour, ushered into

France the prototype of a hero that was to influence the works of generations of writers. It was precisely in 1802, the year Chateaubriand's *René* appeared, that Nodier published the first of a series of books that follow closely the pattern of *Werther,* namely, *Stella ou les proscrits.* This work, although it appeared in 1802 had, according to Nodier, already been started in 1799, for when Nodier went to Paris for the second time in 1801, he took with him the manuscript of this novel.[7] It is an insignificant work and does not appear in many editions of Nodier's works, not even in the *Oeuvres complètes* of Nodier published by Renduel between 1832 and 1837. It is, like *Werther,* an epistolary novel composed of short chapters. Stella, the heroine, in true Wertherian fashion, commits suicide out of retribution for having been unfaithful to her husband in exile. In a minor way, it is also a veiled attack on Napoleon. Of this early work, Nodier admits that it is far from being a success; in fact, he goes so far as to call it a "detestable" book and hopes that it will be "the last bad book I will write." [8] Charles Weiss, Nodier's lifelong friend, and to whom this statement was made, wrote in a letter to the publisher Pertusier on 1 December 1802: "*Les Proscrits* is Nodier's favorite genre for the time being, but it is not his only one. In a few years, when time will have matured his ideas, and if he works hard, I am sure that he will take his place among our most esteemed writers." [9] Unfortunately, Nodier wrote a few more sentimental romances of this type in the years that followed. Yet, despite its limitations, *Les Proscrits,* together with the works that immediately followed, already contain the seeds for the later and more mature works of Nodier. To these early works belong *Le Peintre de Saltzbourg, journal des émotions d'un coeur souffrant* (1803), *Essais d'un jeune bard* (1804), and *Les Tristes ou Mélanges tirés des tablettes d'un suicide* (1806). The two other works, although written during that period, do not belong to the *Wertherian* group; they are Nodier's *Pensées de Shakespeare* (1801) which reveals quite markedly the profession of faith of a Romanticist and indicates quite clearly the author's interest in and admiration for Shakespeare; and *La Napoléone* (1802), an attack against Napoleon and which landed him in jail. Nodier, referring to this work in a letter to Weiss dated 4 January 1804, says that: "A work against the First Consul, written in a moment of exaltation, escaped my pen. Fathers of families have been persecuted for it. I then ad-

mitted my guilt which brought me imprisonment and misery." [10]
(Nodier, even in his later years, liked to give the impression that
he was being persecuted for clandestine political activities.) Two
further works, *Thérèse Aubert* (1819) and *Adèle* (1820), because
of their mood, subject matter, and, above all, because of the date
of their *composition*, have been included in this cycle.

### III  Le Peintre de Saltzbourg (*1803*)

*Le Peintre de Saltzbourg* bears even more markedly than the
earlier work the stamp of *Wertherism* with respect to its form and
its subject matter. It is also reminiscent of Rousseau's *Julie ou la
nouvelle Héloïse*. The story, written in the form of letters, is simple and already familiar. Charles Munster, a painter and poet,
loves Eulalie who, in turn, loves Charles. And if fate were not at
all times interfering with the destinies of men, this story would
have an easy and simple solution. Except that Charles disappears
and is believed dead. Thus, the disappearance of a lover, the appearance of another man, Spronck, and a dying mother, change
the course of events and propel the characters into a melodramatic involvement and denouement. As in *Atala* (1801) a dying
mother's wish has to be respected and Eulalie marries Spronck.
Eulalie bemoans this outcome, especially when she discovers that
Charles is alive and well and has come home to claim her. In one
of her mournful duets with Charles, she deplores her destiny:
"This is how, pitiable heritage of misfortune and death, I became
the bride of another man; this is why I betrayed your memory: to
obey the call of nature and a voice from the tomb." [11]

The influence of *Werther* on *Le Peintre de Saltzbourg* is
both explicit and implicit, and Nodier is not reluctant to discuss
this influence in his preface. Referring to the impact of German
Romanticism on French literature, Nodier says that "the influence
of German literature began to make itself felt in France long before its philosophy";[12] a little further on, referring specifically to
this influence on his own work, he remarks that his work "is a
pastiche of a German novel";[13] and about his hero, Charles, he
says that "he is twenty; he is a painter; he is a poet; he is German.
He is exactly the kind of man with whom I had identified at that
age." [14] Although similarities between *Werther* and *Le Peintre de
Saltzbourg* abound, there are also marked differences, especially
in the domain of esthetics. The most noticeable difference lies in

the portrayal of the characters. Whereas Werther and Lotte never appear ludicrous in their relationship with each other or with other people, Charles and Eulalie often appear so. One of the most melodramatic scenes in the book occurs when Charles sees his beloved outlined in an illuminated window and notices that "She was suffering, for she was looking up toward the heavens. Her bosom seemed heavy, her hair was dishevelled; she put her hand to her forehead, undoubtedly it was burning hot." [15] There are other marked differences. In *Werther* we understand and feel the great and despairing love Werther has for Lotte. This is so because Werther is presented as a more substantial, sensitive, and intelligent individual; Lotte is portrayed as a charming, sensible, sensitive, and intelligent girl who participates in living, who has her hands full taking care of her younger brothers and sisters, and who is always willing and ready to help others. She is not so inextricably involved with herself not to be able to get involved with others. Compared to Werther and Lotte, Charles and Eulalie are but pale and insignificant imitations who cannot really love. Furthermore, although both Charles and Werther are disillusioned with life and with society, Werther is imbued with a greater maturity and strength and his despair and ultimate suicide emerge from strength rather than from weakness or simply because a pattern has been set and must be followed. Thus, Werther's death has a greater impact on us. It is this very maturity coupled with his ability to reason and argue intelligently that comes in conflict with his feelings and his total commitment to emotion and passion. And it is this very conflict that gives *Werther* its tragic quality. It is precisely the lack of this conflict that makes the work of Nodier a melodrama. Totally disillusioned with the world and with himself, Charles is one-dimensional and simplistic in his approach to life and one suspects that his despair and disillusionment reside more in words than in actual experience. One has the feeling as one follows the trials and tribulations of Charles and Eulalie that the machinery has been set in motion and that the characters are merely reacting to certain clichés. In a sense, this procedure is in keeping with Nodier's concept of man's relationship to the universe, for to Nodier as to his heroes, man is the "victim" of an "allpowerful fatality." In Goethe's work, although the hero is also confronted with an irreparable loss and is the victim of the cruel forces of nature and society, when he does commit suicide, one feels that it is done after careful reflection and by choice, "without any romantic exaggeration." [16] Werther commits suicide only, as he himself explains, when "nature finds no way out of a labyrinth of confused and contradictory powers." [17] In other words, when the conflict between two powerful and opposing forces cannot be resolved, suicide is a way out.

Suicide is a dominant theme in the works of many Romanticists. It plays a major role in Chateaubriand and Senancour, as well as in Nodier and Goethe. Nodier, more religious and traditional than Goethe, is quite explicit when he says that suicide is a crime against God and nature. "He who kills himself," Nodier has his hero say, "has misunderstood the intention of God." Furthermore, he continues, man's "supreme virtue was to love his fellowmen and his supreme wisdom to endure his destiny." [18] Goethe, more pagan in his beliefs, takes a more understanding and dispassionate view of suicide, and although he may not completely support Werther's defense of suicide, certainly does not consider it a weak and disgusting act as does the husband of Lotte, the Philistine Albert.

IV   Les Tristes ou Mélanges tirés des
tablettes d'un suicide (*1806*),
Thérèse Aubert (*1819*)
*and* Adèle (*1820*)

*Les Tristes,* as the alternate title states, is a "*mélanges,*" a collection of tales, meditations, comments, poems, and so on. To this collection belong *La Filleule du Seigneur ou la nouvelle wertherie, Une Heure ou la vision,* and *Les Méditations du cloître.* From a historical point of view, *Une Heure ou la vision* is the more interesting because it entails a theme that will be more fully developed in his mystical works: resurrection. The hero has been metamorphosed into a madman and an epileptic.[19] When the narrator discovers him, he is lying prostrate on a tombstone portraying extreme despair as well as extreme exaltation. The first words he utters express ultimate disgust and disillusionment with the world and with man: "You are a man . . . and your heart is made like theirs. I do not like the species man." [20] He despairs because he has lost his beloved twice: once when she was taken away from him and forced to marry another, and again when she died from a broken heart. But he is also exalted because he believes that his beloved resides in a star "floating in a pure light" [21] and that he will soon join her. His feverish and fertile imagination is so atuned to his beloved that he is convinced that she appears to him nightly and even feels this "burden of voluptuousness" [22] pressing against him. Although the tale is brief and overly sentimental, it contains the seeds for themes that will eventually take shape in many of Nodier's more mature works: madness and the possession of a sixth sense, which lunatics, children, and poets possess, a gift that will be given to Michel, Jean-François, sister Françoise du Saint-Esprit and many other childlike and simple souls. Already evident is the concept that man, after having cast off that perishable envelope which he calls the body, continues to live on as a pure spirit in a star. This is, of course, the idea Goethe expressed in *Faust* when he describes the realm of the Mothers, an idea that can also be found in the works of Nerval and Gautier.

*Les Méditations du cloître* is a work of very little artistic merit and its interest lies primarily in what Nodier has to say about monasteries and convents, a topic that was also of interest to Chateaubriand. Nodier, although by no means condemning the cloistered life of priests and nuns, nevertheless, considers reprehensible the idea of entering a monastery or a convent purely as a way of escaping from the responsibilities of life and from one's destiny. This, he says, is almost as bad as suicide. The following is an analysis of the nature and causes of the *mal du siècle* and is reminiscent of the statements Musset and Vigny made thirty years later:

There is a whole generation for whom political events have taken the place of an Achillean education. It was fed on the marrow and the blood of lions; and now that a government, leaving nothing to chance and circumscribing the future, has restricted the dangerous development of its faculties, now that Popilius' narrow circle has been drawn around this generation and it has been told, just as the Almighty told the ocean's tides: "Thou shalt not exceed these limits," do we know to what extent these idle passions and repressed energies can be detrimental to society? Do we know how prone to crime can be an impetuous heart afflicted by boredom? I am saying it with bitterness and with horror; Werther's pistol and the executioner's axe have already decimated us!

THIS GENERATION RISES UP AND DEMANDS CLOISTERS.[23]

In *La Filleule du Seigneur,* a young girl, dying from that malady called "the vagueness of the passions," talks about her wish to enter a convent in order to "bury her youth because society was importunate and because she found life difficult and long." [24] Unquestionably, Nodier admired those institutions where, he felt, tradition, morality, virtue and justice, characteristics long lost to the outside world, are still preserved. Thus, what Nodier is condemning here is not the actual life in monasteries or convents with its secluded life, its devotion to the glory of God and to good works, but the false uses to which these institutions were put by disillusioned and anguished youth. In this condemnation Nodier was not alone. Chateaubriand in *René* also condemns the constant agitation and the "vagueness of the passions" so prevalent among Europeans who, in their agitation and vagueness, "are obliged to build for themselves places of solitude"; [25] in this work Chateaubriand also condemns René's sister for entering a convent in order to bury her terrible secret.

After 1806 Nodier ceased to publish any *contes* or *nouvelles* for some time. The world of the imagination, the dream, gave way to the world of reality. In 1808 Nodier married his Désirée and devoted much time to the establishment of a household and the procurement of the finances with which to run it. Thus, much of his intellectual energy went into the writing of literary and scientific articles, the preparation of lectures for his courses in philosophy, literature, grammar, and natural history at Dole in 1808 and 1809. In 1812 and 1813 he became librarian as well as director of the French-speaking newspaper published in Laybach (Ljubljana). The years 1818 to 1820 saw the publication of three works of fiction: *Jean Sbogar* (1818), *Thérèse Aubert* (1819), and *Adèle* (1820). Although published approximately sixteen years after the appearance of *Les Tristes,* the last two works, because of their subject matter and their mood, justify being added to those works belonging to the Wertherian cycle. This link is further justified by Nodier himself, who says in his "Nouvelle Préface," written for the publication of his *Oeuvres complètes,* that

the short novel, *Adèle,* is, like *Le Peintre de Saltzbourg,* much earlier than *Jean Sbogar,* although it appeared a year or two later. The influence of my early readings is easily found there again, that is, the imitation of the German sentimental novel known to us then only through dull translations; it is Werther, placed in another situation and, unfortunately, speaking a language other than that of his sublime author. . . he has been metamorphosed from the madman of Goethe into an epileptic.[26]

An additional factor comes to the fore to further justify this inclusion: the letters Gaston writes in *Adèle* are dated 1801. More importantly, the heroes are afflicted with the same "vagueness of the passions" that had afflicted Nodier's earlier heroes and heroines. For Gaston, "with his straightforward but very exalted disposition, was unable to defend himself against the influence of that paradoxical spirit with which whole generations were imbued." [27]

*Thérèse Aubert* deals more specifically with the Revolution of 1789 and its aftermath. The hero, Adolphe, does not suffer solely from the *malaise* that had afflicted whole generations; he has, after all, also suffered very directly and very personally from the revolution. The terror that inevitably occurred after 1789 pursued the hero as it haunted Nodier. In this work, Adolphe joins forces with the Royalists. He is alone in the world, his parents having succumbed to the terror. Furthermore, his two teachers, who had eagerly embraced the cause of the revolution, also become its victims. Monsieur Aubert, the father of Thérèse, who gives Adolphe, disguised as a girl, shelter and food, is, in the opinion of Nodier, "too honest a man for these people," [28] that is, for the revolutionaries; he, too, an ardent revolutionary, is eventually swallowed by the very cause he has served. It is, indeed, interesting to note that almost all of Nodier's revolutionaries, if they are portrayed in a favorable light, usually succumb to the cause they had espoused. He is sympathetic to the plight of revolutionaries such as Buonarotti because he sees in them a certain dignity, modesty, and gentleness[29] as well as a sense of humanity. If he condemns the slaughter and terror of the revolutionary government of 1793, he is equally harsh in his judgment of the Directory with its counterterrorism that came into power in 1795.[30] Although a supporter of the monarchy, Nodier did not completely close his eyes to the weaknesses and follies of the Bourbons. After 1824, when Charles X ascended the throne of France, and whose coronation he attended with Hugo in an official capacity, Nodier must surely have become aware of the increasingly repressive measures undertaken by that government.

Whereas *Adèle* belongs exclusively to the Wertherian cycle, *Thérèse Aubert*, because of the special predicament of the hero and because of the date of composition, can also be linked to the theme of the generous outlaw. Indeed, Adolphe, though still lacking the traits of the generous outlaw, namely his contempt, daring, pride, generosity, cruelty and, above all, the terrible feeling of solitude and apartness, is, nonetheless, an outlaw, loyal to the side that has lost power, and, as such, can be regarded as a younger and not yet developed brother of Jean Sbogar.

# CHAPTER 3

# The Generous Outlaw

## I Historical Background

ALTHOUGH published in 1818, Nodier states in his *Prélimi-naires* that *Jean Sbogar* had been "sketched in 1812 in the area which had inspired it," [1] that is, in Illyria (Serbo-Croatia) where he spent the period between December, 1812, and September, 1813, as librarian and as director of the French-language newspaper *Le Télégraphe Illyrien* in Laybach (Ljubljana). Historically, Illyria, as well as other parts of Austria and Italy, had come under the domination of the French around 1809; Laybach became the governmental and administrative seat for the French Empire in Illyria and published its own newspaper. Nodier arrived in Illyria shortly before the defeat of the *Grande Armée* in Russia. After the defeat of Napoleon, the French government, together with its newspaper and its director, were forced to vacate the city and move to Trieste.

In *Préliminaires* Nodier devotes a number of pages attempting to defend himself against the accusations of plagiarism leveled against him. According to the Royalist newspaper *La Quotidienne* (with which Nodier later collaborated for a number of years), two works that had served Nodier as models were Heinrich Zschocke's *Aböllino, der grosse Bandit* (1794) and, in particular, Byron's *The Corsair* (1814). Thus, Nodier's claim that he had already written the first draft of *Jean Sbogar* in 1812 is of paramount importance to his defense. "*The Corsair*," says Nodier, "resembles many things, as will everything written between now and the end of time. But I simply cannot (and I pay my compliments to Byron), find the slightest similarity between it and *Jean Sbogar*." [2] And, Nodier concludes somewhat angrily, "*Jean Sbogar* is neither by Zschocke, nor by Byron, nor by Benjamin Constant, nor by Madame de Krüdena; it is written by me." [3] To this statement one might add that Jean Sbogar, the outlaw, was, according to Nodier, based on a real outlaw by the same name who lived in Illyria and fought against the imperial forces that were subjugating his people: Austria and France. More importantly, the idea of the generous outlaw was very much in the air at the time. R. Maixner in his book entitled *Charles Nodier et l'Illyrie* maintains that "the theme of the mysterious brigand, cruel as well as a dreamer, was a favorite subject between 1810 and 1840." [4] Indeed, the theme of the generous, noble, and mysterious outlaw has played a major role in literature as well as in legend. Both the popular mind as well as the literary mind has concerned itself to a considerable extent with the rebel who challenged the establishment and fought for the underdog against all odds. He was, of course, the pariah par excellence, the outcast of society, a condition self-imposed or imposed upon him by others. He was a figure with whom the writer as well as the ordinary man could identify, especially if he fought and died for such noble principles as justice, freedom, and honor. Although primarily a product of the Romantic temperament, the idea of the noble and generous outlaw goes further back than Schiller and the *Sturm und Drang* period of the 1770's. One of the most popular outlaws who immediately comes to mind is, of course, Robin Hood who, with his loyal followers, lived in the depths of Sherwood Forest, eating the venison of the king which they "washed down with draughts of ale of October brewing"; but who also fought for virtue, honor, and justice. Originally written in the form of ballads in the late Middle Ages, it is no accident that these ballads were turned into numerous prose versions during the nineteenth century. Often the generous outlaw is a dispossessed son on whom an injustice has been perpetrated. Shakespeare's plays are filled with dispossessed dukes, princes, and kings. In *As You Like It* the dispossessed duke lives in the Forest of Arden with his fellow exiles. Similarly, Orlando, ill-treated by his elder brother after their father's death, becomes heir to the animosity that had existed between his father and the new duke, simply because the former had supported the exiled duke. He, too, has to flee the ill-humor of the usurper and, by joining forces with the banished duke becomes, in a sense, an outlaw.

It is, however, primarily with Milton's *Paradise Lost* that we see the origin of the idea of the generous outlaw, for with Milton, Satan "assumes an aspect of fallen beauty, of splendor shadowed

by sadness and death." [5] For in Milton's Satan we already have
the type of hero-villain that became so popular with the gothic
novel and that gave rise to the type of generous outlaw which saw
its beginnings in Schiller's *Die Räuber* (1781). This play, together
with Zschocke's romance *Abällino*, may have, indeed, influenced
the work of Nodier. (In the work by Zschocke we witness not
only the idea of the generous outlaw but also the idea of a double
personality in the hero.) Karl Moor in *Die Räuber* can be considered the prototype of the noble, courageous, generous, and passionate outlaw, who demanded justice for the oppressed and freedom from any established order. Similar to *As You Like It,* sibling
rivalry plays an important role in the development of the play and
in precipitating its denouement. Through the machinations of a
younger brother, a father disowns his favorite son, Karl, without
ever questioning the authenticity of a letter in which he was informed of his son's extravagant and even criminal behavior. Karl,
who also does not question the authenticity of a letter purported
to be from his father, collapses morally when he discovers his
father's extreme reaction to the accusations leveled against him.
With hatred and despair in his heart, Karl turns against the whole
human race and, with the support of a number of followers, becomes a robber and murderer, taking on the whole establishment.

Byron's corsair, Conrad, is also a Romantic desperado; he, too,
has been warped by life and society and becomes an outlaw. The
crimes and injustices that have been committed in the name of
man and humanity have made a villain out of him. He, too, becomes a solitary figure, "exempt from all affection and from all
contempt." [6] Byron's corsair is, like Schiller's robber, brave, loyal,
proud, defiant, and passionate. He is, above all, a free man who
abhors the yoke of the conqueror, the Turk, which makes his reason for becoming an outlaw considerably more valid.

A few years later, Balzac, Hugo, and Stendhal also contributed
to the gallery of generous and noble outlaws. In Balzac's *Les
Chouans,* the "chief of the brigands" is the marquis de Mon-
tauran, also "nicknamed *le Gars*," who fights for king and church
during the civil war that tore France apart after the Revolution of
1789. Hugo's Hernani, who is really Don Juan d'Aragon, becomes
an outlaw to avenge an injustice committed against his father. He,
too, is generous, noble, brave, loyal, tender and passionate. His
sense of honor is perhaps his greatest flaw and leads him to his

doom. In Stendhal's *La Chartreuse de Parme,* the idea of the generous and noble outlaw is perhaps less obvious as theme. Two individuals, Ferrante Palla and Fabrice del Dongo, do, nevertheless, fit the prototype of the generous outlaw. Palla, physician, poet, lover, admirer of Napoleon, and a Renaissance man par excellence, is also an outlaw, for he is under the sentence of death. It is he who helps Gina Sanseverina commit her acts of sabotage and sedition against the Prince of Parma. Palla, however, differs from the other outlaws in that Stendhal has surrounded him with an *opéra bouffe* setting, thereby giving him a comic, swashbuckling appearance. Fabrice del Dongo, generous and noble to a fault, is an outlaw for a while, especially after he has accidentally killed the lover of Mariette. He, too, takes on at times, a certain comic opera aspect, especially when, with his red wig, he pursues the singer Fausta. Like Palla, he is an admirer of Napoleon.

## II   Jean Sbogar (*1818*)

*Jean Sbogar,* as we have seen, was conceived, if not written, during a period in history when Europe was suffering under the yoke of a multitude of tyrants: the Hapsburg and Ottoman Empires, Napoleon, and the many petty tyrants that existed throughout Europe and the Middle East. Jean Sbogar, like Conrad in *The Corsair,* was an outlaw in a country where liberty was not yet a reality; like Conrad, he belonged to a society where men could still be good and noble, or so it was believed by those who were disillusioned with their own society and who felt that to be generous and noble was no longer possible in the more civilized societies of Western Europe. That is why almost all the outlaws belong to nations considered exotic at the time. Sbogar fought against the tyranny of the Hapsburg Empire as well as the Napoleonic Empire, a period when Napoleon, with his *Grande Armée,* occupied much of Serbo-Croatian territory. Thus, in a sense, Sbogar was wanted simultaneously by the soldiers of two occupying forces. In Nodier's work, as in that of Byron, the outlaw is a political outlaw, a national hero, who is rebelling against an imperial power and who is trying to instill into his people a national consciousness.

The rebellion on the part of the small nations of Europe and the occupation of much of Europe by the *Grande Armée* of Napoleon poses a special problem. It is, indeed, strange and paradoxical to discover that under Napoleon, ideas on freedom, equality, and justice were actually being introduced by the soldiers of Napoleon into those countries that were rebelling against local or foreign tyrants. Moreover, the members of the *Grande Armée* saw themselves not merely as occupier but also as liberator and, in many instances, the French government often sided, although covertly, with the indigenous population, often supporting, at least morally, many of the rebel leaders, especially if these leaders were rebelling against a major power to which France was not favorably disposed. (In this case it was Austria.) Such sympathy was apparently extended to the people of Illyria. *Le Télégraphe Illyrien,* which Nodier directed for a while, was to serve not only as mouthpiece for France and French culture and inform the French-speaking public of the events that were taking place in Europe, but also to gather and disseminate information and material about the local area: its history, poetry, legends, language, dialects, and so on. The unofficial policy of the newspaper was to express French revolutionary ideas on equality and freedom. According to Maixner, Fouché, one of the governor generals, was to have directed Nodier to do just that: "Bring out the advantages of French influence on public education, speak about the abolition of fiefs, speak about liberty; it is a word that sounds good in all languages." [7] This policy should come as no surprise when one considers that one of the chief concerns of Napoleon was to bring together the two great divisions of France: the *ancien régime* and the spirit of the Revolution of 1789. It should be remembered that many of the soldiers of the *Grande Armée* were veterans of the revolution and had fought for the revolutionary government against the foreign coalitions that had been formed expressly to break the backbone of the revolution. These soldiers were still inspired by revolutionary ideas. (This policy of revolution abroad does, indeed, contradict the rigid control of the press and free speech that existed within France itself.)

When one compares *Jean Sbogar* with the works of other writers on the same theme, one is immediately struck by the complexity of this work, with its many social, political, and philosophical arguments (especially those presented at the end of the book as the *Tablettes de Lothario*), and, above all, by the portrayal of a rather complex and interesting human being. For in *Jean Sbogar* the hero has a double personality: he is Jean Sbogar the rebel and national hero, the outlaw, who is wanted by the authorities; and he is Lothario, a nobleman, gentle, sensitive, who, on occasion, comes to Venice where he has a palace. Lothario is respected by all and lives alone, cut off from all but his servants. He is very liberal with the poor and the sick and greatly loved by them. He meets and loves the beautiful and rich Antonia and, in turn, is loved by her. And, one would suppose that all is well. Both are rich and Antonia has the consent of her older sister, her guardian and sole companion. But when Antonia meets Lothario she experiences a strange feeling that they have met before; it was ."something vague, blurred, and obscure, which had the nature of a reminiscence, a dream, or an attack of fever." [8] Antonia's feelings of uneasiness and foreboding are, of course, quite valid. A few months before her arrival in Venice, while sleeping in the forest, she had been awakened by the voices of two men, one of which belonged to the outlaw Jean Sbogar; and the voice she heard uttered these strange words:

My being links itself to her, hovers over her, don't you see, following her in this brief life, in the midst of all the ambushes set by men or fate, without her being aware of me for a moment. She is my conquest for eternity; and since I have lost my existence, since I have been forbidden to share it with such a sweet and noble creature, I am taking hold of her for all eternity. I swear by the sleep that she is now enjoying that her last sleep will reunite us and that she will slumber near me until the earth comes to life once again.[9]

Lothario is also the heir to the sorrows of Werther and René. He, too, suffers from the *mal du siècle*. Already at an early age he had been disillusioned by civilization and the idea of progress and had sought refuge in the mountains of Montenegro where he had lived in blissful freedom and solitude with the Montagnards, away from the vicissitudes and the evils of society. For two years he had been happy until the day foreign troops invaded the land. It was the subjugation of a free people that transformed Lothario into Jean Sbogar. Soon Jean Sbogar became the head of an organization that called itself the *Frères du bien commun*. With his fellow outlaws he performed feats that were good and bad, as is usually the case in a guerrilla war. Above all, they freed political prisoners and fought against the injustices perpetrated by a conqueror on a subjugated nation; they also devoted themselves to the elimination of poverty. These ideals and principles won for

the group, and especially for Jean Sbogar, the respect and the
support of the local population, which consisted primarily of the
lower classes. They also aroused the fear and hatred of the upper
classes who were usually on the side of the occupier. Thus Sbogar
became a Herculean figure and had the power to frighten whole
battalions of government soldiers into retreat by merely showing
himself to the enemy. And, says Nodier, "simple men, always en-
amored by marvels, embellished his life with episodes that were
most singular and diverse." [10] It is obvious that the idealistic moti-
vations of this clandestine organization were considered subversive by the authorities and the more popular Jean Sbogar became,
the more brutal and ruthless became the soldiers of the government. This, in turn, led to acts of brutality on the part of the
rebels. Nodier makes a very astute observation about the syn-
drome of political uprisings and the outlaws who were shaking
the various countries and governments at the time.

Almost all of them were prompted by the most generous sentiments
and guided by the purest devotion; but behind them a league came
into being, composed of violent men for whom political disorders were
only an excuse, and dangerous to all governments and disavowed by
them all. Sworn enemies of social laws, they openly led to the destruction of all established institutions. They claimed to be for liberty and
happiness, but they marched, followed by arson, pillage, and murder.

Despite Lothario's frequent disappearances from Venice and
the sudden ambushes and meetings with Jean Sbogar, the two
sisters never suspect that Lothario is Jean Sbogar. On occasion,
whenever the conversation centers around the outlaw, Antonia
and her more conservative sister condemn the actions and beliefs
of Sbogar. To Antonia, Sbogar is a tyrant fighting against law and
order, causing fear and unrest among the population. Nonetheless, the name of Sbogar, mentioned in the conversations of the
rich or uttered on the lips of an old man singing a song that de-
picts the terrible plight of his fellow countrymen, causes Antonia
to become pensive and troubled and anticipate the final meeting
with the legendary figure.

Besides telling the story of a generous and noble outlaw and his
love for a young girl named Antonia, *Jean Sbogar* also presents
numerous discussions about God, religion, and death; it also gives
us the famous *Tablettes,* a sort of testament or profession of faith

of Lothario/Sbogar. The concept of the *néant*, of nothingness, and *l'anéantissement*, the act of entering into the void and merging with the universe, was a concept that fascinated and frightened many Romanticists. A quotation by Friedrich Klopstock, German Romantic poet (1724–1803), on *l'anéantissement*, introduces a chapter which deals with death and the idea of the *néant*. Indeed, interest in Klopstock on the part of Nodier is not of recent origin and goes back to *Les Proscrits* and *Le Peintre de Saltzbourg*. (Charles Munster, as well as Werther and Lotte, also greatly admired the German poet.) Lothario, in his affinity for philosophical disquisitions and in his complexity of character, is much closer to Werther than he is to Nodier's earlier heroes who were paler imitations of Werther. Already at an early age Lothario found himself vacillating between conflicting ideas: a need to believe in immortality and a skepticism which made such a belief impossible. Thus Lothario's skepticism and disillusionment led to a belief in the *néant* and *l'anéantissement*. In his desire to find God, Lothario could find only "doubt, ignorance, and death." [11] Only the pure, Lothario felt, could find God and immortality, because God "has given the prescience of immortality to pure souls for whom immortality is created. However, to those souls whom he has destined in advance for the *néant*, he has only shown the *néant*." [12] Like all Romanticists, Lothario expresses "an immense void" which is akin to the *mal de l'infini* of Pascal and the existential nausea of the Sartrian hero. Lothario is, of course, *l'homme fatal* whose destiny has been mapped out by some greater force or power. When Lothario explains these ideas and emotions to Antonia, she feels the terrible horror of being confronted with the *néant*, that is, eternal nothingness, which to her is akin to eternal damnation. "What," she cried out, "beyond this life that so rapidly runs out . . . nothing! nothing for him! the *néant?* What is the *néant?* and what is eternity if Lothario is not there?" [13]

In the end Jean Sbogar is captured and executed after Antonia, who had been requested to identify him, finally realizes that the Lothario she had loved so desperately was the Sbogar she had so desperately feared. Thus, in death, the young nobleman who loved and was loved, becomes one with the outlaw who also loved Antonia but who feared even more the purity of his beloved. It was this very purity and his fear to besmirch the innocence of their love, a love that had been made in heaven, that prevented Lothario from marrying Antonia; the specter of Sbogar was forever present. Thus neither Lothario nor Sbogar would ever share a bed with Antonia on this earth.

Although Antonia discovers the true identity of Lothario, this identity is never made public. Sbogar dies, as Nodier says, "under the obscure name of a simple Montenegran adventurer." [14] Maixner, in his appraisal of the hero Jean Sbogar, pays him the highest tribute when he says: "how much more ardent, more carried away, more dynamic Jean Sbogar seems to us . . . compared to this pale René who appears to be disillusioned about everything without yet having tasted anything." [15] The fact that Jean Sbogar was not merely an imitation of characters in literature but was based on a flesh-and-blood individual who had fired the imagination of Nodier as well as that of a nation, may have contributed to the success of the work. And Nodier's annoyance with the many reviews of his book which compared his work with that of Byron, Zschocke et al., is understandable.

### III   Les Tablettes

Just as Lothario and Sbogar are united in death, it is also in death that the fictitious Sbogar becomes united with the real Sbogar. Like his fictitious counterpart, the real Sbogar was, according to the testimony of Nodier, a man of great charm and nobility, and a polyglot. Moreover, Nodier tells us, the *Tablettes*, which he inserts in the work, are based on statements made by the real Sbogar in conversations Nodier had with the outlaw and which he purports to document with scrupulous veracity. These *Tablettes*, presented in the form of *pensées* similar to those of Pascal and which Lothario gives to Antonia before parting from her, introduce us to Lothario's ideas on government, freedom, slavery, capital punishment, and which are undoubtedly ideas also held by Nodier. This assumption is based on what Nodier stated in his new preface to *Adèle* written in 1832:

I did not belong to the liberal party, because I loved liberty too sincerely to do so, and the act of faith that I made to liberty in the *Tablettes of Jean Sbogar* were not the kind that would reconcile me with those official legatees who have always conceived of liberty in a different way than I have.[16]

In his *Préliminaires* to *Jean Sbogar* Nodier explains that several
pages were later added to the *Tablettes* which had been eliminated for political reasons from the 1818 edition. What those political reasons were and why these precautions had to be taken in
1818, are not made clear. We do, however, know that Nodier in
his youth had belonged to secret societies, that he most likely was
a Freemason and, perhaps, even a member of the Carbonari; it is
equally true that Nodier liked to give the impression that he was
involved in conspiracies and that the publication of the *Tablettes*
involved certain risks. What is, however, clear is that the *Tablettes*
are also Nodier's profession of faith.[17]
On liberty, equality, and government:

A tired and worn-out nation asks to be governed. A depraved nation
needs to be subjugated. Liberty is a generous source of nourishment
and is only fitting for a healthy and robust adolescence.[18]

When politics become mere jargon all is lost. There is one thing that
is more vile than the slave of a tyrant, that is the dupe of a sophist.

It is inconceivable that men cut each other's throats for their rights
and that these so called rights of man are merely mystical words interpreted by lawyers. Why does one not speak to man about the first
right of man, that is, his right to a part of the earth in proportion of
the individual to the territory.

What kind of law is this which bears on its brow the name and seal
of equality? Is it the agrarian law? No, it is the contract of sales of a
nation that has been sold to the rich by the intriguers and partisans
who want to become rich.

It is frightening to think that equality, which is the object of all our
vows and of all our revolutions, becomes a reality in only two states of
man: slavery and death.

Few men can bear the sight of seeing a proud lion in an iron cage
licking humbly the bloody hand of the butcher that feeds it without
shuddering with indignation and sorrow. What must man think who
looks at man?

I would like to be shown in history one monarchy not founded by a
thief.

Liberty is not so rare a treasure: it is found in the palm of the strong
and in the purse of the rich.

There are deep in the heart of man three errors or three mysteries which permit him to live: God, love, and liberty. And society would not have existed for 2000 years if some beggars from Galilee had not decided to found a religion on them.

I have sometimes been asked if I loved children. Of course I do. They are not yet men.

On crime, the criminal, and capital punishment:

It is difficult to decide what is more hideous in society: crime or the law, and who and what is more cruel: the guilty one or the judge, the crime or the punishment. Opinions in this matter differ considerably.

To kill a man in the paroxysms of passion, is understandable; to have him killed by a civil servant and with the solemnity of a sacred rite is not understandable.

A society that kills a man is indeed convinced that it is just. What an immense and sublime retribution of justice the man who kills society!

Two crimes exist for which I have no pity: to hurt those who cannot defend themselves and to steal from those who are in need. Torment and malediction on him who steals a dog from a blind man.

What difference is there between a crime and a heroic action, between torture and an apotheosis? The place, the time, the despicable opinion of the stupid crowd which does not know the true meaning of things, and which looks upon chance rather than habit as the prime mover of occurrences and events.

A great number of these ideas will be expressed once again in many of Nodier's tales. This is especially true of Nodier's condemnation of capital punishment which is evident in *L'Histoire d'Hélène Gillet*. In the following tablet we already witness the Nodier of *La Fée aux miettes* wherein he extolls the virtues of the simple, humble life of a carpenter.

If my heart could believe . . . and if I had a God to invent, I would want him to be born on straw in a manger, to escape his assassins only in the arms of a poor artisan, serving as his father, that his childhood be spent in misery and exile; that he be an outlaw all his life, despised by the great, unknown to monarchs, persecuted by priests, betrayed by friends, sold by one of his disciples, abandoned by the judge with the most integrity, sacrificed to torture in preference to the worst of scoundrels, whipped, crowned with thorns, outraged by the executioner, and that he perish between two thieves, one of which follows him to heaven.

Most powerful God, have pity on me! [19]

The most interesting idea to emerge from this tablet is the idea of Christ as an outlaw, perhaps the outlaw par excellence who, with his followers, fought against the yoke of the Roman Empire.

### IV   Mademoiselle de Marsan (*1832*)

Although *Mademoiselle de Marsan* was published in 1832, its setting and subject matter justify its being placed with *Jean Sbogar*. However, compared with *Jean Sbogar*, *Mademoiselle de Marsan* is inferior and its heroes lack the complexity and passion of the generous and noble outlaw, Jean Sbogar. It has, nonetheless, a historical interest in that it also includes a portrayal and discussion of a secret society, the Carbonari.

The action takes place around 1808 and also deals with national heroes rebelling against the yoke of a foreign government. The narrator is once again Maxime Odin, a naturalist, who spends some time on the shores of the Adriatic and who is also hiding from the police for having taken an interest in the "noble resistance of nations against the invasions of Napoleon." [20] Maxime also gets involved with secret societies and with the daughter of a French officer, Diane de Marsan. In Venice he meets Mario Cinci, the Doge, a Roman by birth, and leader of the movement that seeks independence from the foreigner, Austrian as well as French, and favors the restoration of the old republic of Venice. In his attempt to gain independence from Hapsburg, Cinci makes a pact with Napoleon. But it is an uneasy pact, for the secret society of the Carbonari is no more permitted by Napoleon than it is by the Austrians. The second part of the book is devoted to other rebel leaders: André Hofer, a peasant leader from the Tyrol, Joseph Solbioski and Dr. Fabricius. All three are linked to Mario Cinci and his independence movement. Also linked to this movement is Mademoiselle de Marsan who loves and is loved by Mario Cinci. Unlike Antonia, Diane embraces the activities of her lover and follows him into exile. However, at the end of the second part we discover that both she and Mario have drowned. In the third part Maxime Odin and Joseph Solbioski are at the Torre Mala-

detta, the domain of the former rebel leader, Cinci. This part is
somewhat reminiscent of the gothic novel with its dungeons and
steep precipices, the discovery of a dying Diane and her dead
servant in one of the many dungeons, and the final escape. In the
end the liberation movement disintegrates. Solbioski is captured
and executed; Hofer and Fabricius are sought by the Imperial police. In 1808 Napoleon's *Grande Armée* is still victorious. However, although the leaders are caught and killed, the organization
of the Carbonari continues in its attempt to change the political
picture of Europe.

## V   *The Carbonari*

The formation of clandestine societies was an attempt to
change society, for many believed that reform could only be
achieved through covert, subversive activities. These secret societies, nationalist in temper, were undoubtedly one of the most
important agents of political and social change in the early nineteenth century. In various countries in Europe Freemasonry became one of the instruments of political awareness and ferment,
especially among the bourgeoisie. This was especially true in Italy
where the secret societies sought ferment and rebellion against
the Hapsburg Empire and the Napoleonic Empire. The most important nationalist secret society in Europe was the Carbonari,
which was especially active during the first three decades of the
nineteenth century. The Carbonari borrowed their name from the
guild of charcoal burners and woodcutters just as the Freemasons
had borrowed theirs from the guild of the masons. The first lodges
of the Carbonari were founded between 1802 and 1810 by a
group of Republican officers in the French army who were hostile
to Napoleon. Many Freemasons were also members of the Carbonari. But whereas the Freemasons were primarily an ethical
and social group, a fraternity intent in helping the brotherhood,
the Carbonari were essentially a political and nationalist organization. The function of the Carbonari was to stir up opposition to
the French army and government of occupation in foreign lands
and to press for constitutional guarantees. The members of the
Carbonari were not only against Napoleon, but against tyranny in
general. They tried to instill a strong feeling of national consciousness among the various oppressed peoples. Although their support
came primarily from the middle classes, support also came from

disaffected officers and soldiers. It was the Carbonari who supported the cause of liberalism against the Holy Alliance set up
after 1815 to control Europe; it was the Carbonari who won a
constitution for Spain and for some Italian states and independence for Greece; it was the Carbonari who were behind the Deka-
brist uprising against Nicholas I of Russia in 1825; and it was the
Carbonari who were instrumental in furthering the revolutions
that spread throughout Europe in 1830.

But the society of the Carbonari was also an ethical and social
organization and its members swore to help their brothers as well
as their families in case of need. Like the Freemasons, they had a
body of beliefs and rituals which they swore to keep secret. It is
primarily this aspect of the Carbonari and the Freemasons, their
attempt to instill solidarity among the *compagnons,* the Brothers,
as well as reintroduce the old moral and ethical values, that held a
particular appeal for Nodier and which he discusses in his article
entitled *De la Maçonnerie et du Carbonarisme* (1833). The Carbonari, Nodier felt, more than the Freemasons who had lost track
of their original purpose and intent, continued to teach industry
and honesty and all the other virtues to the people, basing their
teachings on a Christianity that was tolerant, free, and compassionate, a Christianity that was revolted by all excesses.

The dogmas of the Carbonari were simple and striking, their mores
were grave and exemplary, their rites embodied a natural majesty
which could be imitated only imperfectly. The Carbonari never ex-
hibited a charity that was overtly brilliant; rather, a veritable spirit of
brotherhood existed, all the more sincere and effective because it was
animated by a consciousness and a need for reciprocity which was
understood by all and which maintained with a perfect exactitude a
generous sympathy among all the members of the order. Even the title
of *cousin,* less emphatic and compulsory than *brother,* gives the extent
of this loyal and modest kinship which did not promise so much but
which was all the more assuring.[21]

And it is this spirit of spontaneity, freedom, simplicity, and equality that made the Carbonari "spread under the reign of Napoleon,
the seeds of ferment." [22] Nodier then discusses the importance of
the Carbonari in Italy and their alliance with similar fraternal and
student organizations in Germany. Nothing, says Nodier, is "more
noble and more touching than the movement of a generous popu-

lation that rises against an internal tyranny or against a foreign
invasion." [23] Nodier sees secret societies such as the Carbonari and
the Freemasons serving an important function in furthering the
moral, religious, and political order of a nation, assuring its freedom and curtailing the greed and ambitions of tyrants. Thus the
social and ethical values of secret societies, their ability to sow
ferment againt tyrannies, his own pessimistic view of man and
society, progress and perfectibility, his interest in the occult, account for Nodier's propensity for secret societies, making him join
early in life the *Méditateurs* and the *Philadelphiens* and support,
if not join, the Freemasons and the Carbonari.

# CHAPTER 4

# *Demons of the Night*

## I  *Historical Background*

CASTEX refers to the period between 1820 and 1822 as the "cycle frénétique" of Nodier, the period when he, like so many others, came under the influence of the gothic novel and vampirism. The 1810's and 1820's do, indeed, represent a period when the "genre frénétique" reached its apogee and when the fantastic became steeped in morbidity and aimed at achieving a "frisson de l'épouvante" through the introduction of vampires, ghouls, ghosts, werewolves, and other such creatures. According to literary historians, it was Byron who was the prime instigator in arousing interest in vampirism, a phenomenon that appealed greatly to his temperament. In 1816 Byron, who was writing his *Childe Harold* at the time, was in Geneva with the Shelleys, Dr. G. G. Polidori, and Matthews G. Lewis. "It proved a wet, ungenial summer," writes Mary Shelley,

and incessant rain often confined us for days to the house . . . In the evenings we crowded around a blazing wood fire, and occasionally amused ourselves with some German stories of ghosts, which happened to fall into our hands. These tales excited in us a playful desire of imitation . . . . "We will each write a ghost story," said Lord Byron, and his proposition was acceded to.[1]

The challenge was, indeed, taken up by all concerned. Mary Shelley wrote *Frankenstein, or the Modern Prometheus,* Byron his *Fragment* of a tale of horror, and Polidori, *The Vampyre,* which was later, in 1819, attributed to Byron. The hero of this work is Lord Ruthwen, a Byronesque type, a libertine, who becomes a vampire. He first seduces the beloved of his friend, then his friend's sister whom he marries and suffocates during their wedding night. Thus, a love-crime—self-destruction and the destruction of the women one loves or desires—is an integral part of vampirism. In 1816, with the support of Byron, Charles Robert Maturin was able to produce his play *Bertram* at the Drury Lane Theatre where it was an immediate success. Nodier, with his friend Baron Taylor, translated and adapted *Bertram* for French audiences in 1821; in France, too, it became exceedingly popular. Other influences, especially legends dealing with vampires and werewolves, brought back during the late eighteenth century by travelers from their voyages to Eastern Europe, also played an important role in furthering interest in vampirism. Voltaire had devoted a long article to the vampire in his *Dictionnaire Philosophique*. However, his main concern had been to make fun of vampirism and, in the process, attack those ordinary and very human vampires we meet in the world of business and who "in broad daylight suck the blood of the nation." [2] Goethe in his *Braut von Korinth* (1797) had already exposed the public to legends on vampirism. Articles about the world of the nightmare, of which vampirism is simply an outward manifestation, also appeared in the various newspapers and reviews and contributed to this interest. Nodier, very much interested in vampirism and the "genre frénétique," wrote in 1819 a review of Polidori's *Vampyre* for the Royalist newspaper, *Le Drapeau Blanc*. In this review Nodier links vampirism and the frenetic with the moral state of society; he sees in this type of literature a need on the part of a blasé generation to experience sensations that are "outrageous, turbulent, and convulsive," and to experience them "at all costs." [3] In almost all of his discussions of the "genre frénétique" we come across a conflicting attitude on the part of Nodier: an attraction to the type of literature that expresses strong and fearsome sensations and the need to condemn it, which is primarily dictated by the general attitude of his more conservative peers. Most important, however, is the fact that Nodier demonstrates a keen understanding for his age and an appreciation for the type of literature that was a natural outgrowth of this age. Writing for *Les Débats* on 1 July 1819, Nodier says:

The legend of vampirism is perhaps the most universal of all our superstitions. . . . It is, indeed, a strange phenomenon to see simple, natural men, the least likely to deceive one, savages who have nothing to gain from an alleged illness, confess to vampirism and accuse themselves, with horror, of this involuntary crime they commit during their sleep. . . . The terrible malady I am talking about is called Smarra in Slavic. It is probably what we call a nightmare in French.[4]

In 1820 *Lord Ruthwen ou les Vampires* was published in two volumes and bore the initials G.B. Since it included Nodier's *Observations préliminaires* it was assumed that Nodier was also its author. After much discussion about authorship, it was revealed that the "culprit" was Cyprien Bérard. Further investigation revealed that the work was a French adaptation and translation of Polidori's *Vampyre* and intended to be a sequel to it. In his *Observations* on this novel, Nodier evinces once more a degree of reticence and hesitation with respect to the frenetic in literature and says that literature should be approached gingerly and soberly; but this does not prevent him from presenting that same year a melodrama entitled *Le Vampire* written in collaboration with Carmouche and Jouffroy and which was based on *Lord Ruthwen.* In 1821 Nodier published *Smarra,* a tale about vampirism but in which the vampire no longer is a man who destroys himself and another human being, but a supernatural dreamlike being. *Smarra,* together with Byron, influenced the works of other writers. Hugo, with his *Han d'Islande,* presented, in 1823, vampirism, satanism, and, for that matter, even the theme of the outlaw. That same year vampirism was also evident at the Théâtre de Gaîté where a gothic pantomine entitled *Polichinelle vampire* was performed. Étienne-Léon de Lamothe-Langon published in 1825 his hybrid novel *La Vampire ou la Vierge de Hongrie,* which attempts to mix chivalry with the frenetic in the manner of the gothic novel. In 1827 Mérimée published a collection of stories, ballads, and popular songs entitled *La Guzla* which purported to be of Illyrian origin and wherein the "genre frénétique" and vampirism are prominently present; his *Lokis,* written in 1869, also deals with vampirism—in this instance the hero is a young Lithuanian count who, on his wedding night, bites the throat of his bride. In *Carmilla* (1871), Sheridan Le Fanu masterfully presents gothicism, vampirism, and lesbianism. As late as 1897, another Irishman, Bram Stoker, terrifies his readers with vampires and werewolves in *Dracula.* The cinema, not to be outdone, has, from its very inception, been fascinated by vampires and werewolves. Roman Polanski's *Fearless Vampire Killers* (1967) is only a recent attempt to deal with an old familiar theme.

## II   Smarra, ou les Démons de la nuit (1821)

During and since his sojourn in Illyria, Nodier wrote many articles on Slavic literature and language. His enthusiasm was so great that he even led people to believe that there existed a collection of Illyrian poems and songs which he hoped in time to translate and publish for the benefit of the French public. When *Smarra* first appeared, the public was informed that this work was of Illyrian origin and had been translated by Maxime Odin. In his preface Nodier also informs the reader that the word "smarra" means "nightmare" as well as "vampire" in the Slavic dialects and that Dalmatia was one of the main seats from which many legends on vampirism emanated.

A short résumé of *Smarra* will, I think, reveal the intricacies of the tale and indicate to what extent and in what manner this tale differs from the usual tales of vampirism that were so popular during that period. The tale is divided into five parts. Part 1, the prologue, describes the sensations and thoughts of falling asleep; a young man, Lorenzo, sings his joy at being once again united with his beloved Lisidis, whom he is holding in his arms, and praises the delights of this reunion; but he also reveals the terrors of the night that haunt him during his sleep. In Part 2, we are suddenly transported from pleasant Lombardy to a somewhat sinister and nightmarish Thessaly. Lorenzo, suddenly stripped of his identity, has become Lucius and is riding through the night, the victim of his own hallucinations brought about by his immense fatigue. Sensual images of young girls lulling him to sleep soon give way to images of spectral figures among whom he discovers his friend Polémon. This surprises him because he had only recently seen his friend die in battle. Closely following upon the heels of Polémon is a fearful pack of demons and sorcerers.

In Part 3, Polémon begins his tale of how Méroé, the sorceress, delivered him to Smarra, the demon of the night, whom she loved and carried in a magic ring. In Part 4, it is again Lucius who tells how he, too, fell into the clutches of Smarra. Lucius is now accused of the murder of his friend, Polémon, and is condemned to death and beheaded. As in a veritable nightmare, Lucius sees his own head rolling on the platform, and he is conscious enough to observe Polémon have his heart torn out by the couple Smarra and Méroé. In Part 5, Lucius, who has been transformed back into Lorenzo, wakes up from his nightmare, reassured by the presence of his beloved and relieved that he had merely been visited by the demons of the night. He also discovers that he has a cramp in his arm which he got holding his beloved in his arms.

Although much of the work of Nodier had already come to the attention of a sizable public, it was primarily with *Smarra* that he made a name for himself. But this does not mean that the tale was well received. Despite the attention given to *Smarra* by critics and readers, the tale was completely misunderstood, for the public expected another straightforward, traditional type of tale dealing with vampires, ghosts, ghouls and sorcerers. Misunderstanding the intent of the tale, the critics and readers complained that it was obscure, vague, and filled with digressions, inconsistencies, and distracting details that had little to do with the plot. Indeed, Nodier, well aware of such a possible misunderstanding, had warned the reader in his preface that to understand *Smarra* "one must perhaps have experienced the illusions of the nightmare which this poem faithfully recounts." [5] Aware that his warnings had not been heeded, Nodier, in a second preface, declared that "these characters are precisely those of the dream, and whoever resigned himself to read *Smarra* from beginning to end without realizing that he was reading a dream, took needless trouble." [6]

It is precisely this attempt to simulate a dream or, rather, a nightmare, with its inconsistencies and digressions, its incoherences and absurdities that makes this tale so markedly different from the usual tales of vampirism and terror of the time. Indeed, *Smarra* is unique and considerably ahead of its time in its attempt to give the impression that it is a dream and that, like a dream, it is composed unconsciously, as though the narrator were writing in a trance. It is, of course, reminiscent of automatic writing, a technique the Surrealists tried to develop one hundred years later. It is because of this tale that Nodier can be considered an important initiator in attempting to record the impact of the dream on man's psyche and, above all, on the psyche of the writer, as well as its use in literary creation, an aspect that was totally ignored by the critics of the day. These important factors are stated clearly in *Smarra:*

The poetic life of a man is divided into two series of sensations more or less equal and of similar value, one of which is the result of the

illusions of man's waking life, the other is shaped by the illusions of
sleep. I will not argue about the relative merits of one over the other
of these two ways of perceiving the world . . .

What astonishes me is that the poet in the waking state has so
rarely profited in his works from the fantasies of the poet in the sleeping state or, at least, that he has so rarely acknowledged that he has
borrowed from them.[7]

Nodier is, however, very much aware that at least one poet had
been able to comprehend the importance and impact of sleep and
the dream on man's psyche and their use in literature: Shakespeare. In a footnote to *Smarra* Nodier discusses the relationship
between the cramped position of one's body (which had precipi-
tated Lorenzo's demons of the night) and a nightmare in Shakespeare's *Tempest:*

In the *Tempest* of Shakespeare, the type of creation that cannot be
imitated, *the man monster,* who is devoted to the evil spirits, also com-
plains of the terrible cramps that he has just before dreaming. It is,
indeed, strange that this physiological inducement of one of the most
cruel maladies which torments the human species has only been
grasped by poets.[8]

Although the publication of tales and plays dealing with vampires, werewolves, ghouls, and ghosts was extremely successful at
the time, many critics and reviewers of conservative magazines
and newspapers did not share this enthusiasm and were critical of
the "genre frénétique" and considered it to be in poor taste.
Above all, these critics maintained, this type of literature was foreign to the French classical mind, and an importation from across
the Channel and the Rhine. *La Quotidienne,* a newspaper primarily devoted to the defense of throne and altar, praised *Smarra* as
it had previously praised *Jean Sbogar* although its editors were
basically opposed to Romanticism and the "genre frénétique."
What they liked about *Smarra* was that it was picturesque and
harmonious. No doubt the editors of *La Quotidienne* were misled
by the classical setting and wanted to say something nice about
one of their collaborators. (Nodier worked closely with *La Quotidienne* between 1821 and 1824.) Perhaps Nodier's preface contributed to the favorable attitude on the part of some conservative newspapers, for in this preface Nodier declares that he got the

idea for *Smarra* from *The Golden Ass* by Apuleius, a work which
even the most rabid anti-Romanticist would have to consider classical. Indeed, similarities between the two works are considerable,
although the intent, as Maixner points out, differs; *The Golden
Ass*, after all, is a satire *against* sorcery. But, we ask ourselves,
why allude to this classical work? Did Nodier, fearing, once again,
to be accused of plagiarism, wish to ward off his accusers by beat-
ing them to it? According to Maixner, Nodier alludes to Apuleius
in order to make obvious the link between this *classical* work and
its use of an exterior fantastic, and his own use of the "genre
frénétique" which was considered by conservative critics as the
most extreme and reprehensible kind of Romanticism. Thus, Nodier
is implying, if a classical writer is allowed to portray grotesque
and bizarre creatures and the supernatural with impunity, so can
he and other Romanticists. In its battle against Romanticism, *La
Quotidienne*, like so many other Royalist newspapers, vehemently
opposed the "genre frénétique" because the editors saw in this
type of literature a covert expression of political and social anarchy and believed that if they condoned the new ideas and
trends in literature, they would soon be forced to accept the new
social and political ideas. The domino theory was already in existence at the time. An article by one of the editors of *La Quotidienne*, Mély-Janin, dated February 19, 1821, expresses the typical
attitude of the conservative Royalist press. Raving against the foreign influences that were infesting France and French literature at
the time, the drama critic of *La Quotidienne* says: "It is high time
that we oppose these invasions of the barbarians. For some time
now the armies of Romanticism have crossed the Rhine and the
Thames, and burst on to our scene; and now they wish to conquer
by force, the rights of the city." [8]

### III   Trilby, ou le lutin d'Argail (*1822*)

It may astonish some to find that as charming a tale as *Trilby*, a
tale where the themes of the dream and love are so delicately and
nostalgically drawn, is placed in that category of tales which come
under the heading of "demons of the night." But chronology and
subject matter dictate, in part, that this be done. Just as there is a
link between the noble and generous outlaw and the vampire, in
that both destroy themselves and the one they love, so is there a
link between the vampire and the little will-o'-the-wisp, Trilby,

that charming little troll or goblin. Needless to say, this tale, too, differs considerably in mood and intent from the tales of vampirism and the horror stories (gothicism and *Schauer-Romantik*) so popular during the period. In this tale the cruel, greedy, and destructive vampire has given way to Trilby, the *"feu follet,"* a charming little sprite who takes as his abode the stables, the hearths, and the cracks in the walls of manors and huts. In return for shelter he does little chores around the house, helping a milkmaid fill her bucket of milk or insuring that the fishing is good. He is also a charming prankster who likes to annoy "the old women who speak ill of him in their vigils or to trouble the sleep of young girls and women with incomprehensible but charming dreams." [9]

It was considered a great honor to have Trilby choose one's hut or manor as domicile. The ladies of the manor and castles grieved that Trilby had not chosen them. But Trilby was in love with Jeannie, the wife of Dougal, the fisherman. As she sat alone, dozing before the hearth, her spindle lying idly in her hand or as she slept at night, he would whisper his love for her and remind her that "the dreams you like best, those in which you see a child caressing you with love, I myself send them to you and I am the child whose lips, enflamed by these sweet marvels of the night, are pressed by yours. Oh! realize the happiness of your dreams!" [10] And Jeannie, in all her innocence, enjoyed the little games that Trilby played; she liked these gentle flatteries, these innocent but voluptuous dreams. She enjoyed the illusions that were afforded to her "in this space of uncertainty between rest and the waking state when the heart, despite itself, remembers the impressions that it had tried to repress during the day." [11] But those terrible impressions and sensations that are forced unwittingly upon one at night, the very ones which one tries to suppress during the day, have a way of making trouble! Such is the fate of Jeannie. Such also is the fate of Madame Bovary, for example. Having a romantic temperament, Jeannie, like Madame Bovary, conjures up a world suited to her own needs and desires. She is less daring than Madame Bovary, perhaps because she has a more vivid imagination, perhaps because this "cancer of lyricism" has not yet been thwarted by a humdrum existence; the romantic setting of Scotland may have been kinder to a romantic spirit than the setting of Yonville.

Soon Jeannie, in her honesty and simplicity, uncorrupted by civilization, begins to worry. She worries especially when at times "she thought she felt the pressure of an agitated hand, the ardor of a burning mouth." [12] She reveals to Dougal what she considers to be impetuous seductions by the demon who loves her. Without much ado, Dougal calls on the old monk Ronald, who comes to the hut with his sacred books. Thus, with the help of prayers, relics of saints, the sacraments, the holy litanies, the Virgin and Solomon on the one hand, and the *Rituel* and *Clavicule*, books on sorcery and demonology, on the other, Ronald exorcises Trilby, threatening to imprison him in a tree for a thousand years should he ever try to return to the hearth of Dougal. After the capture of Trilby things are no longer the same. Jeannie becomes agitated and morose. Wondering whether Trilby has not found a new hearth or a new love, she even becomes jealous. Dougal no longer catches the fine, large blue fish. The nights, like the days, have now lost all their charm. What is even more serious, in her jealousy, her nights have become less and less peaceful. When she finally does sleep, she dreams no longer of Trilby in the form of a charming little child. Rather, Trilby has become a handsome, elegant youth: "They were the fine and delicate traits of the will-o'-the-wisp but developed into the imposing forms of the chief of the clan of the Mac-Farlanes." [13] Furthermore, jealousy and a sense of guilt have emboldened Trilby's amorous ardor, for "the glances of Trilby no longer contained that frank expression, the candid confidence of happiness. The smile of a thoughtless innocence no longer played upon his lips." [14] In short, with Trilby becoming more human and sensual, their relationship has lost its first innocence. Jeannie now knows that in this new form "she could only take a guilty interest, and deplored his exile without daring to desire his return." [15] Torn between guilt and repentance, on the one hand, and suppressed desires over which she has no control, on the other, Jeannie experiences anxiety and moroseness. As long as her imagination was allowed free play, the images evoked were free and innocent. But as soon as an attempt to suppress them was made, guilt appeared, and the images took a more sensual form.

The love Jeannie has for the will-o'-the-wisp is a dream she has created for herself. The relationship, the conversation, between Jeannie and Trilby reveal the torments of persons who are sexually frustrated, who are forced to sublimate the demands of their sexual desires, and who are compelled to escape into a world of the imagination where dreams are permitted and act as a safety valve, a sort of compensation for these frustrations. Jeannie, like Nodier's later characters Michel, Jean-François les Bas-Bleus, Baptiste Montauban, all live in another dimension, namely that of the subconscious, or unconscious, of the dream, where their secret torments, their instincts are laid bare, and where they are seemingly safe from outside interference, unless it be their own guilt, as is the case with Jeannie.

The characters may be lost in reveries, rather than in nightmares, tales such as *Trilby* may have the grace, the charm, and the delicacy reminiscent of fairy tales and old legends, rather than tales of vampires, yet their very tone, even their form, is deceptive. The demons of the night are as active in these reveries as they are in nightmares. Trilby, the little demon of the night, has a more charming, a more subtle appearance, but, underneath it all, he is the little brother of the vampire, and can destroy as voraciously and as effectively the one he loves. Jules Janin was well aware of this link between *Smarra* and *Trilby* when in February, 1832, he wrote in the pages of the *Revue de Paris:* "Shake hands, Smarra and Trilby. Happy is he who has found Trilby or Smarra, Smarra or Trilby; but much too happy is he who has found simultaneously both Trilby and Smarra." [16] Thus, Smarra is the nightmare, the dream that oppresses and suffocates; Trilby is the dream or the reverie that consoles and cajoles one, at least temporarily. But both are demons of the night; they are the two sides of the same coin. Both are troubling in that they reveal suppressed needs and desires. Whereas with Smarra the attack is direct, with Trilby, the attack is oblique and has merely the appearance of innocence and is thus all the more perfidious.

Trilby was greeted with as little enthusiasm and understanding in 1822 as *Smarra* had been in 1821. Nodier sadly refers to this lack of understanding on the part of critics in his preface of 1832. The main target was the verisimilitude of the locale. According to the *Edinburgh Review,* Nodier's description of the locale in no way concurred with the real surroundings. But in view of Nodier's preference for the imagination, the dream, it is clear that he cared not a whit about reality, that, on the contrary, a remark such as this could only give him great pleasure.

As for me, I was looking only for the delightful lies in place of which they put their erudition and their reason from which they will never get joys similar to mine. Anyone who will follow down the Clyde then go up Lake Long towards the Cobler, leading Trilby by the hand on some beautiful summer day, will be able to verify the sincerity of my descriptions. They will merely appear less poetic than nature itself; this is my fault.[17]

Like most Romanticists, Nodier preferred the imaginary voyage to the real one. Nonetheless, Nodier did undertake a trip to Scotland which he recorded in *Promenade de Dieppe aux Montagnes d'Écosse*. Scotland, with its mountains and vales, its lakes, its seas, with its fogs and mists, its castles and abbeys, its pagan background superimposed upon Christianity, served Nodier as an ideal place where he could allow his imagination free reign. He picked this remote region primarily because its people had managed to retain an innocence and simplicity that had already disappeared in more sophisticated areas. Reflecting on the lack of "delightful lies," [18] of interest in the supernatural and the occult, he says:

We have progressed too much to enjoy those delightful lies and our hamlets are too sophisticated today for us to use them as appropriate settings for interesting old superstitions. One must run to the far corners of Europe, confront Northern Seas and Polar ices to discover in semi-savage huts some tribe entirely isolated from the rest of mankind and able to move us by its touching errors, and who are the sole vestiges of the age of ignorance and sensibility.[19]

When, however, by 1830, the *conte fantastique,* with its stress on an interior, psychologically oriented, fantastic, became fashionable, *Trilby* finally became successful. It is perhaps appropriate at this point to mention that decades later a historian named Jules Michelet discovered our little will-o'-the-wisp, Trilby, hiding in the hearth of a lonely and imaginative woman, her spindle lying idly in her lap, dreaming of another and better world to which she could escape, and devoted a chapter to "the little demon of the hearth" in his book entitled *La Sorcière* (translated into English as *Satanism and Witchcraft*).

IV   Les Aventures de Thibaud de la Jacquière (*1822*)

This short tale, published in 1822, first appeared in a small volume entitled *Infernaliana,* a collection of tales dealing with demonology, sorcery, and black magic. This edition contained the initials C.N. which immediately followed the words "published by." According to Castex, it is not clear who wrote these tales; it is, however, certain that almost all of the tales included in this anthology were not written by Nodier, but were merely collected by him from other sources and then published by him. Castex, however, by including this tale in the 1961 Garnier edition of Nodier's works, seems to imply that the tale was actually written by Nodier. Marcel Schneider in *La Littérature fantastique en France* says that five of the tales are by Dom Calmet who, in 1751, had written a *Traité sur les apparitions.* According to Schneider, one of these tales is *La Nonne sanglante,* which is taken from Matthews G. Lewis' *The Monk.* Interest with respect to the authorship of this tale has been considerable. In a preface to a 1958 edition of John Potocki's work entitled *Manuscrit trouvé à Saragosse,* Roger Caillois states that *Les Aventures de Thibaud de la Jacquière,* reproduced and somewhat amended in the 1822 edition of *Infernaliana,* was actually the text of an episode found in the Potocki novel. A few years later, Jean Decottignies, writing for the *Revue des Sciences Humaines* in 1963, verified the Potocki source and pinned it down to the chapter dealing with the tenth day of the life of Alphonse van Worden. This tale, says Decottignies, was, in turn, influenced by a tale of the seventeenth-century writer François de Rosset.

*Les Aventures de Thibaud* deals with a young renegade named Thibaud who makes a habit of getting drunk and, when drunk, of challenging the devil to come and get him. One evening when he is out walking, trying to clear the fog in his head, he meets a young girl accompanied by a little black dwarf. They look lost and, indeed, they are lost, for the little dwarf had fallen and broken their lantern. Thibaud, although a renegade, is still gallant and offers to escort them to their house. Arriving at the house, Thibaud is invited in for supper and, to his good fortune, to the bed of the pretty Orlandine. However, when he is ready and eager to embrace the pretty maiden, instead of finding in his arms a voluptuous and seductive girl, he feels the claws and sees the terrible features of Beelzebub. Beelzebub had finally heeded Thibaud's challenge. In this tale, the demon of the night is, indeed, a real demon and not the charming little will-o'-the-wisp, Trilby, who loves Jeannie and who, because of his love, brings about the downfall of Jeannie as well as his own. Neither is this demon Smarra, nightmare or vampire. Moreover, this tale is reminiscent of the much longer work of Jacques Cazotte entitled *Le Diable amoureux,* an eighteenth-century tale that influenced a host of French and German writers: Hoffmann, Nodier, Nerval *et al.* It should perhaps be pointed out that *Le Diable amoureux* also parallels to a considerable degree Nodier's *Trilby.* In the Cazotte work the devil, Biondetta, a beautiful and charming girl, does, indeed, fall in love with the hero Alvare whom she has been ordered to tempt. When she finally, out of love, gives herself to him, she brings about her own downfall.

After 1822 the creative adventure of Nodier came to a standstill, at least for a while. Much of his work between 1823 and 1830 was devoted to articles and book reviews published in newspapers and magazines. It was during this period that Nodier became librarian to the Duke of Artois at the Arsenal and where he opened his salon to the literary lions of the day. The years between 1824 and 1828 were a period that was socially brilliant and marks Nodier's very active official role in the history of Romanticism. But by 1827 the salon at the Arsenal began to decline. Debts, poor health, his break with Hugo, the revival of the Cénacle at the home of the Hugos, and the engagement and marriage of his beloved daughter, Marie, contributed to the deterioration of the sessions at the Arsenal, as well as to the decline of the health and financial status of Nodier. To make matters worse, Nodier also lost his position as librarian and with it the pension that was his main means of support. Once more the physical and tangible world of Nodier begins to shrink; once again Nodier feels compelled to turn to the world of the imagination, the dream, the world of the creative adventure, for solace and comfort.

# CHAPTER 5

# *The Cycle of the* Voyants *and the Innocents*

ALREADY in such works as *Smarra* and *Trilby*, it became apparent that the nocturnal dream, which is that state which occurs during sleep, as well as the diurnal dream, the state which approximates the dream and when an individual is more cognizant and creates a world of his own, a state Asselineau called *la double vie*, had taken a firm hold on Nodier. This world of the dream continud to influence Nodier with an ever increasing intensity after 1829. For Nodier now considered the dream of paramount importance to the psychic health of man and, by extension, to his own psychic life and survival. The nocturnal dream, Nodier felt, was a means of knowledge, of insight, a way of entering another world, the *au-delà*, the beyond; the dream also brought to the surface certain suppressed desires and aberrations, a phenomenon he had already described in *Smarra* and in *Trilby*. In an essay entitled *De Quelques Phénomènes du sommeil*, written in 1830, Nodier attempts to analyze in detail the phenomenon called sleep and its impact on the psychic life of man and the poet.

## I *The Nocturnal Dream*

In this essay Nodier discusses the impact that sleep has on man's waking life and the development of faculties unknown to him heretofore. Sleep, to Nodier, is the most powerful, the most lucid state of man's mental life and opens a door to the discovery of beauty and wisdom. It is through sleep and its accompanying dreams that religions have come into being and kingdoms have been founded and saved. In biblical times the patriarchs often made decisions on the basis of what had been revealed to them in their dreams.

The first perception that dawns through the inexplicable dimness of dreams is as clear as the first ray of sun dissipating a cloud, and the intelligence, hovering a moment between the two states dividing our life, quickly lights up like the flash dazzlingly jumping from the sky's tempests to the earth's tempests. It is then that the immortal conception of the artist and of the poet flashes; . . .[1]

Nodier then goes on to discuss the nightmare which he describes as a common occurrence in sleep, particularly to those who have a vivid imagination: children, passionate young people, and those who have much idle time.[2] Atheists, according to Nodier, never have nightmares because they lack imagination, the ability to believe in the marvelous, the unknown. Religion stimulates the imaginative faculty; conversely, religion is the creation of the tremendous imagination of man. The intensity of the nightmare is thus in direct proportion to the vividness of the imaginative faculty.

Anticipating Freud, Nodier says that dreams are often the overt expression of a monomania, an aberration, of desires that are suppressed and fears that are latent. Two factors, which medical philosophy should investigate, are of paramount importance to an understanding of monomanias.

The first one is that the perception of an extraordinary act, unusual to our nature, is easily converted into dreams; the second, that the perception of a recurring dream is easily converted into acts, especially when the dreamer is weak and irritable.[3]

In this connection Nodier cites two examples of monomanias: a hypothetical one, and one with which he had direct experience. With respect to the former, he discusses the fears a shepherd may experience, namely, the fear of wolves, a fear that is quite understandable. However, this fear may take gigantic proportions and become so deep-seated that the shepherd may dream that he himself has become a wolf in search of the very lambs he must protect. The other example deals with the personal experience of a young painter whose mistress had died from starvation and misery. Before dying, the poor woman had implored him to eat her so that at least he might survive. When the narrator meets the painter, he is the victim of a recurring nightmare in which he digs up the interred remains of his beloved in order to eat them. This, Nodier says, is an example of a werewolf, and to say that this phenomenon does not exist would be a great error and misunderstanding of man's psyche. Aberrations of this sort, continues Nodier, do, indeed, exist and are an integral part of the psychic life of man, his other self, his "bête fauve." Nodier goes one step further. Not only do dreams reveal man's terrors and monomanias; these very dreams can, according to Nodier, serve as a means of curing these very aberrations:

it seems to me that this theory, thoroughly studied by a philosopher, would not be useless for the treatment and cure of most monomanias, these probably being but the prolonged perception of a sensation acquired in this fantastic life, which represents half of our life, the life of man asleep.[4]

Dreams expressing certain monomanias or aberrations, dreams that reveal suppressed desires and thoughts and latent fears, are, indeed, abundant in the works of Nodier, revealing, perhaps, not only the obsessions and desires of the fictitious dreamer but, also, those that may lie within the creator of these works. Nodier's obsessions with executions, with bloody, severed heads, feature very prominently in his works. This has already been noted in *Smarra*. An execution is also the chief event in *Histoire d'Hélène Gillet*. References to executions are also made by the outcasts of society, those "innocents" such as Baptiste Montauban or Jean-François les Bas-Bleus who foresees the death of Marie-Antoinette. In *Trilby* the heroine has dreams that reveal her suppressed desires and fears.

## II   *The Diurnal Dream*

Rare is the man who does not have two lives, one that, for convenience's sake, he calls "real," usually humdrum and prosaic, often filled with fear and anguish, and a world of the imagination, a world of the dream, shaped to fit his ideals, his demands, his needs, a world rid of tensions, of the burdens of space and time, a world in which one does not grow old or die, a world which permits escape and hope and which defies the human condition. It is this world, the dream world of the *double vie*, which is basically composed of the same elements as those which one experiences during sleep, that Nodier also stresses in his works.

Living in a world filled with injustice, without values and morals, a world of rootlessness and opportunism, of quacks and cads, Nodier felt that the world of the dream was of paramount importance to the survival of his mental stability. The world of the dream, that important part of the *double vie,* is that

sweet state of the mind where it isolates itself at will from all realities of life, where it can alienate itself without any loss from the past, the present, and even from experience, to create a world of its own choice upon which it exercises with sovereign authority all the attributes of God's power.[5]

Here Nodier is no longer referring to the dream one experiences in the sleeping hours, but is alluding to the dream that one experiences when one is awake and cognizant and which permits one to enter a world of thought that is more voluntary and controlled, a state where the imagination reigns supreme. It must be pointed out that Nodier was very much aware that for the dream to be effective and satisfying, the dreamer had to be productive, that is, the dream had to be transformed by work, by the creative act, into a work of art. Nodier feared that the dream itself, a delicious and consoling liar,[6] could easily lead to inactivity and stagnation. However, by writing his *contes fantastiques,* Nodier prevented his dreams from vanishing. In his preface to *Les Quatre Talismans,* Nodier discloses to the reader the reason why he writes:

The *Nouvelles* that I tell myself before recounting them to others have moreover a charm that consoles my mind. They divert my mind from realities and let it exercise upon chimeras of my own choice; they occupy it with dreamy and lonely ideas which move it or with cheerful fantasies that amuse me; they let me lead a life which has nothing in common with the ordinary life of men, a life which separates me from them a little less than I would like, but as much as it is possible for the imagination to extend its boundary and to go beyond its pale. That is why I wrote my *Contes.*[7]

In *L'Amour et le Grimoire* the narrator confesses to two passions: "to see myself as the hero of a story that is fantastic" and "to write . . . a good story that is fantastic, extravagant, and innocent." [8] His desire to write about and experience the fantastic was so great in him that he was willing to give ten years of his life.

The fantastic, my God! But I would have given ten years of my life, I would have struck a great bargain just to meet a sylph, a fairy, a sorcerer, a clairvoyant who made sense, an *idéologue* who could understand himself; to encounter a gnome with blazing hair, a ghost with a robe woven of fogs, a minuscule sprite, the most minute and simplest of imps that ever hailed on the parsley. . . .[9]

Nodier has said a great deal, not only about the nature of the dream, but also about the nature of the fantastic. He has, as already noted, written an essay on the fantastic in literature, and in almost every *conte*, either in the form of a lengthy preface or prefaces, he has something to say about it. For Nodier, one of the first prerequisites for the creation of the world of the fantastic is a firm belief in it.

In all my life I will not write an *histoire fantastique*, you can take my word for it, if I do not have in it as sincere a faith as in the most common notions in my memory, as in the most daily facts of my life, and I do not believe I lack intelligence or reason any more than the wits who absolutely deny the fantastic. I differ from them, it is true, by a certain way of seeing, feeling and judging, but they differ from me in the same way, and I do not feel obliged by any known and avowed defect of constitution to submit the intimate perceptions of my senses and of my conscience to the whim of a mocking authority whose sole motive for questioning might be a presuming ignorance. America was a fantastic world before Christopher Columbus.[10]

The *histoire fantastique,* according to Nodier, must reach the heart of the listener. To accomplish this, "one must first of all be believable, and . . . to be believable, one must believe." [11] Thus the *histoire fantastique* is a sort of consolation to those who have lost their illusions, a return to a state of innocence, a lost paradise. Furthermore, "the good and genuine *histoire fantastique* of a skeptical age could be suitably placed only in the mouth of a madman," [12] for the madman, living in a state of innocence, in a primordial paradise of his own, can, together with the child, most readily understand the fantastic. It is for that very reason that Nodier lets Michel, whom he meets in a lunatic asylum in Glasgow, tell the story of *La Fée aux miettes*. The *histoire fantastique* is, thus, not for and by academicians and pedants, but for those who have imagination. In his attempt to seek the fantastic in literature, Nodier has tried to discover a new type of fantastic, a fantastic that emerges as a logical outcome of a dying civilization. "What I was looking for," he says in *Smarra*, "several men have since discovered it; Walter Scott and Victor Hugo, in those extraordinary but *possible* types . . . ; Hoffmann within the nervous frenzy of the inspired artist." [13] It is quite obvious that Nodier is speaking here of a type of fantastic that differs considerably from the conventional fantastic filled with ghosts, vampires, and werewolves, although he does not completely shun these elements. Neither is he referring to the mysterious or to fantasy, for both these types are too optimistic in tone. Rather, he is referring to the type of the fantastic introduced by Hoffmann, a fantastic that is an integral part of the narrative, namely, the *fantastique sérieux* or the *fantastique intérieur* which occurs in the psychic life of man. It is a fantastic that "comes to the surface like the dream of a moribund," [14] and from which it acquires its dreamlike quality. Since the dream is also comprised of the bizarre, the morbid, the macabre, even the mad, often the result of suppressed desires, it is quite natural that the *conte fantastique* should duplicate these qualities. The *conte* or *histoire fantastique* frequently portrays the nocturnal life of man and gives the impression that it is narrated in the state of sleep or semisleep, a sort of dream within a dream.

In *Histoire d'Hélène Gillet*, Nodier discusses three types of the fantastic. First there is the "false *histoire fantastique* whose spell results from the dual credulity of the teller and of the public, as in Perrault's *Contes de Fées*." [15] Then there is the "vague *histoire fantastique* which leaves the soul hovering in a dreamy and melancholy doubt, lulls it like a melody, and soothes it as a dream." [16] To this group belongs the delightful story of *Trilby*. The third type is "the genuine *histoire fantastique*, the best of all, for it deeply moves the heart without asking any sacrifice of the reason." [17] This third type of the fantastic has the strange quality of being "considered materially impossible but which nevertheless happened in the eyes of all the world." [18] To this third category belongs the *Histoire d'Hélène Gillet*. Nodier's *La Fée aux miettes*, his most delightful work, contains elements of all three.

### III   La Fée aux miettes ( *1832* )

*La Fée aux miettes* starts out very much in the way that Diderot was wont to begin his works ( *Le Neveu de Rameau, Jacques le*

*Fataliste*). It is a dialogue between the narrator and his valet on the topic of lunatics, which will serve the narrator as a point of departure in ridiculing certain ideas about lunatics that were current at the time. The valet is prosaic and believes in reality. To prove the validity of something (in this instance it is the reasoning power of the Eskimos), he says: "I believe it . . . just as I believe in the brush and the topcoat of *monsieur* that I have just folded on the desk." [19] In *La Fée aux miettes,* Nodier expresses his recurring theme of the fusion of the nocturnal and the diurnal life. All the characters who come in contact with the Fée aux Miettes have great difficulty in differentiating between these two worlds. And this applies also to the hero, Michel: "Alas! I said to myself, my whole life is but a chimera and a caprice, ever since the Fée aux Miettes is involved." [20] At first Michel fears the impact of the world of illusions, of dreams, on his daily life. But gradually, through the aid of the Fée aux Miettes, he becomes, together with his creator, convinced that the world of the dream is liberating, that the dream "liberates consciousness from the clutches of the real and plunges it for a while into that state of bliss which is the usual region of innocence or, as it is supposed, of madness." [21]

Indeed, Michel's relationship with the Fée aux Miettes is so bizarre, his quest is so incredible, that, as he himself exclaims, "nobody believes in it, since my faith in events seemingly fanciful in the judgment of universal reason is interpreted as a sign of weakness and of mental disturbance." [22] To the pedants, to the phony scientists, such as the alienist in the lunatic asylum, Michel is indeed deranged, a lunatic who belongs to that group so designated because they show such little concern for the business of the day, who are strangers in the real world, as if they were, indeed, the descendants of the moon, and who talk about things alien to most people. However, to Nodier there is no difference between the world of the dream and the world of madness. Both states are attempts to escape the world of reason. The dream is, after all, but madness that is fleeting; madness is a dream that lingers and continues into the waking hours.

To this group of innocents belong childlike old people such as the nun Françoise du Saint-Esprit (it is surely no accident that she is so named), with her "sweet childlike smile," or childlike children, because they are "in a state of grace and innocence." To this group of innocents belong Jean-François les Bas-Bleus, Bap-

tiste Montauban, also called the idiot, and the woodcutter
Xaïloun, who considers a lizard his beloved cousin. According to
Nodier, they occupy "the highest step in the ladder." [23] They live
in a world of their own making, mainly because they are different,
and being different, they are subject to scorn and ridicule which
in turn forces them to develop a world of their own. Incapable of
hurting anyone but themselves, they are forever the recipients of
vicious and brutal behavior on the part of this "populace
grossière." When Baptiste, who talked to and protected birds, is
discovered drowned, "dead for ever," one of the children, who
thinks like an adult, shouts: "What luck! . . . I know where he
left his Polish cap which, like a nest, is filled with green baby
canaries!" [24]

These idiots, these lunatics, these innocent ones are, of course,
Nodier's preferred characters, being children of the imagination,
of the dream. He wonders whether their lunacy is not really wisdom and feels they are endowed with a sort of sixth sense ena-
bling them to know and see things, states to which the Pharisees
are incapable of attaining. Nodier enjoys confounding, and thereby
humiliating, the dogmatic scientism, the quackery of his day, with
the wisdom and purity of his lunatics. In *La Fée aux miettes*,
Michel emerges as "the most reasonable character," as compared
to the pedantic alienist and quack, "a man who is rigid and severe,
dressed in black from head to toe," [25] who ridicules Michel's search
for the "mandrake that sings." But the pedant fares the worse,
for he is mercilessly ridiculed by Nodier when he has the narrator
mistake the pedant for a madman. Nodier's attack against the
quackery of alienists with their meaningless jargon, who pose as
philanthropists is, according to Castex, based on an article he had
seen in the *Revue de Paris* of May, 1829. In this article so-called
new techniques and methods to cure lunatics are discussed which
he attacks vehemently at the end of *La Fée aux miettes*.

What a marvelous society ours is, in which those two prime individuals,
the one whose life is harmless to others and the one who lives in solitude, are contemptuously thrust to the outer limits of society like the
poor children who died without the benefit of baptism! [26]

The Fée aux Miettes, a mixture of the traditional good fairy and
Nodier's own original invention, and Michel, the carpenter, are

innocents par excellence. The Fée aux Miettes is small like a
child; she is forever losing her money; she jumps about incessantly. According to the carpenter Finewood, she is "a dwarf two
and a half feet tall, several hundred years old, called the Fée aux
Miettes, who speaks all the languages, who professes all the sciences, and who dances according to the latest fashion." [27] In short,
with her deftness at commerce (she does, after all, have a flourish-
ing business with the Levant and, together with Michel, supplies
"the cedar beams and the cypress panelling for the palace that
Solomon is having built for the Queen of Sheba"),[28] her coquetry
and her wisdom, she is the ideal "honnête homme."

In the *Voyage pittoresque et industriel dans le Paraguay-Roux,*
the hero, Kaout't'Chouk, sets out in search of an ideal, namely, the
perfect man whose presence will ensure the perfect society. But
the ludicrous, mock-serious tone of Nodier quickly makes us
aware of the unattainability of the perfect man and, therefore, of
the perfect society, at least as it is conceived by the type of man
which society glorifies. However, in *La Fée aux miettes* the hero,
Michel, is also in search of an ideal, symbolized by the mandrake
that sings and which, as the Fée aux Miettes puts it, "will present
itself of its own accord to the hand destined to pick it." [29] It was
the Fée aux Miettes who sent him on this errand, for the mandrake's powers would prolong her existence and change her into
the young and beautiful Belkiss, the Queen of Sheba, who will
eventually become the widow of Solomon and marry Michel.
Michel finally finds the mandrake in a lunatic asylum where the
director (the one whom the narrator takes for a madman), a man
with no poetry, with no sensibility, finds Michel mad for wanting
to find a mandrake that sings.

What, precisely, are the powers of that flower that Michel
wants so badly? We are told that it will prolong the life of the Fée
aux Miettes and transform her into Belkiss. We are also told by
the narrator that the mandrake is a powerful narcotic suitable for
easing pain and Michel says that the mandrake, through its hallu-
cinatory potentials, can offer solace to the finder "by bringing to
those suffering souls an oblivion that is sweeter than sleep, and
almost as impassive as death." [30] Presumably, this means that it
can give solace to man by fusing the two worlds of experience:
the world of reality and the world of the dream. There is also the
possibility that the mandrake, possessing aphrodisiac qualities,

suggests the desire for physical love when the Fée aux Miettes tells Michel that this mandrake is a "remarkable specific that would lengthen my life by returning my youth to me";[31] for, as has been noted, during their marriage, before Michel sets out in search of the mandrake, the Fée aux Miettes had been very strict about locking her door at night and preventing Michel from entering her room.

But Michel has not yet found the flower which will assure his happiness with the Fée aux Miettes and/or Belkiss and sadly tells the narrator:

. . . It is there, it is in this clump of green and pleasing mandrakes that the secret of my last illusions is hidden; it is there that with the last mandrake, the one with the remaining bloom, the one that will yield to my fingers' last efforts but which will bring no song to my ears, or yours, it is then that my heart will break! and you know how much a man wishes to postpone till the last moment—under the spell of a long-cherished hope—the distressing thought that he has dreamed everything . . . EVERYTHING; and that nothing remains of all his chimeras . . . NOTHING! [32]

Although in an epilogue we discover indirectly that all ends well and that Michel has found his mandrake that sings and is now married to Belkiss, we know that Michel did not really need an outside stimulus to achieve his ideal, that is, to have the Fée aux Miettes merge with Belkiss. For Michel's faith and his imaginative faculty have enabled him to do so without outside aid. In Michel we witness the gradual development of the imagination as he begins to perceive the beautiful young Belkiss in the old Fée aux Miettes. Belkiss, heretofore just a portrait which he cherished and always had with him (with, of course, the tacit approval of the Fée aux Miettes) comes to him on his wedding night. Whether this happens in a dream or in actuality is incidental. Concurrently, Michel also suddenly discovers that his locket contains a second portrait on the reverse side, namely that of the Fée aux Miettes. Thus, the two characters merge more and more, and the two worlds, the world of reality and the world of dreams, begin to fuse. When Belkiss comes to him, she is almost as tall as he is ("that is because I have stretched myself," she replies to his query), has long hair, and is without her two long canine teeth[33] (for which she again has a ready explanation). When Michel

worries about "this uneasy feeling of voluptuousness, this almost
deadly feeling of bliss" which he suddenly experiences when he is
near Belkiss and which he never experienced when he was near
the Fée aux Miettes, she answers: "Oh! Don't let that astonish
you . . . at night all cats are grey." [34] And when in the morning
Belkiss disappears and Michel cries out "Belkiss!" in the hope of
retaining her, he hears the voice of the Fée aux Miettes announcing breakfast.

This same conversation is repeated between him and the Fée
aux Miettes on the eve of his departure to seek the mandrake that
sings. Michel cries out: "These explanations, Fée aux Miettes, I
have dreamed them once before, or I am dreaming them now."
To this the Fée aux Miettes answers: "Oh, don't let that astonish
you . . . everything is truth, everything is falsehood." [35]

In the merging of the Fée aux Miettes with Belkiss, Michel has
found that ideal equilibrium between the two worlds which
affords him happiness. Thus, what Nodier is saying is that happiness, the ideal, is really within us, in our own imagination, in our
ability to dream, and in a strong faith. And this happiness finds
further strength in the sweet joys of work and a simple, wise existence. Two things lead to happiness: to believe and to love; and
Michel had these prerequisites; he never for a moment lost faith
in the Fée aux Miettes and remained faithful to her. Michel is, of
course, like Parsifal and like Pantagruel, in search of an ideal, an
ideal that can only be discovered by the innocent, those with faith
and love who lead simple and wise lives. Surely it is no accident
that Michel, the carpenter, is practicing the best profession in the
world, the very profession that Christ professed.

La Fée aux miettes, itself, contains dreams of every type. On his
wedding night, when his bride, the Fée aux Miettes, locks him out
of her room, Michel dreams that the beautiful Belkiss, the Queen
of Sheba, comes to him. When he spends the night at a crowded
inn in Greenock, he has to share a room with a bailiff from the Isle
of Man. Michel is glad to comply, but he is somewhat discon-
certed at what he sees:

What amazed me . . . was that his shoulders were surmounted by the
magnificent head of a Great Dane and that I was the only one among
mistress Speaker's many boarders to notice it. This embarrassed me
since I did not know exactly in what language to address him and

since I understood only with some difficulty his own. It consisted of a
weak bark, modulated to a low pitch, accompanied by very expressive
gestures. What is certain is that he understood me perfectly well and
that after a quarter of an hour of conversation, I was surprised both by
the clearness of his speech and by the exquisite delicacy of his judgments.[36]

Whether this rather bizarre experience is a dream or not we do
not know. It is part of the fabric of Nodier's work and we must
accept it as a reality or else reject a major portion of his work.
Michel, himself, does not know when one state ends and the other
begins:

I was about to sleep, unless I was already asleep, for to tell the truth,
Sir, my impressions between waking and sleeping are sometimes mixed
up and I never trouble myself much to disentangle them, since I would
not know how to decide exactly which ones are the most reasonable
and the best. I imagine it amounts roughly to the same thing, in the
end.[37]

Neither do we know whether the nightmarish experience Michel
has that same night is real or imagined. For during the night
Michel sees four monstrous heads emerging before him: the heads
of a wildcat, a bulldog, a horse, and a man. They are trying to rob
the sleeping bailiff of his wallet. Knife in hand, Michel rushes at
the intruders, hitting in all directions. In the morning, Michel is
discovered "lying down flat near my bed, the bailiff's wallet in one
hand, and a knife in the other. I was asleep." [38] Near him lies the
immobile body of the bailiff. Michel is arrested and tried, and
Nodier takes the opportunity to satirize justice at its worst.

Understanding a language with which one is not familiar is a
common occurrence in dreams. That animals appear in dreams
with the ability to speak and understand the human tongue is
nothing unusual; and that one understands them is also a common
phenomenon. This ability on the part of animals to speak and
humans to understand that speech is also a common occurrence in
the fairy tale. Nodier is not alone in expressing this idea. Nerval,
in *Aurélia*, has birds and people speak in tongues unfamiliar to
the narrator who, nevertheless, understands intuitively what is being said. Gautier in *Le Pied de la momie* understands Coptic in
his dream although he had never studied the language. He under-

stands the Princess immediately and has no difficulty in speaking
to her in that tongue. This ability goes back to the belief that
religions, myths, the alphabets of peoples, as well as their languages, have a common source. It is, in a sense, akin to the Platonic idea of archetypes. Many Illuminists and with them Nodier,
Nerval, and Baudelaire, also believed in an archetypal, universal
language to which all earthly languages corresponded. The discovery of this universal language, acquired through intuition, is
the key to the mysteries of nature, a key to the world beyond
appearances. This kind of an *Ursprache,* or original language, and
an *Urpoesie,* considers the poet as the one best suited to decipher-
ing and interpreting this primitive language. This notion is, of
course, linked to the idea that the poet is a seer, a diviner.

## IV   *Two approaches to* La Fée aux miettes

Nodier's best-known and best-loved tale, *La Fée aux miettes,*
has caused much controversy and has been the object of many
interpretations. On its most obvious and simple level, it is a fairy
tale for adults. It contains, as we have seen, elements of the nocturnal and the diurnal life of man and is imbued with the sense of
the fantastic and the marvelous. It is, as Castex says, the tale of a
man who is desperately trying to retain a childlike heart and who,
with a childlike faith and innocence, clings to the world of the
dream. Castex has harsh words for those critics who use the psychoanalytical approach in an attempt to interpret the tale. He
considers these critics as pedantic and as foolish as are the pedants portrayed in the works of Nodier and whom Nodier delights
in satirizing.

Albert Béguin sees *La Fée aux miettes* as a myth as well as a
dream wherein Nodier expresses his innermost and secret desires
and passions, and thus enables the author to seek and find a refuge for his alter ego. *La Fée aux miettes* is what the Germans
refer to as a *Kunstmärchen* (an art fairy tale), a form that
reached a high stage of development with E. T. A. Hoffmann.
This type of fairy tale differs from the folk fairy tale or legend in a
number of ways. First, it often takes place in the present era:
Nodier's *La Fée aux miettes* takes place during the author's life-
time, as does Hoffmann's *The Golden Pot.* Secondly, the fantastic
and the marvelous merge with the everyday, prosaic world with
such ease that the reader is temporarily deceived, only to be bru-

tally awakened, thus causing him a strange sense of discomfort as soon as this deception is perceived. We are then immediately shocked out of our complacency and our comfortable feeling that all is well and familiar to us, and are catapulted into a world that is strangely removed from our everyday experience—a world in which the dark forces of man's innermost nature are suddenly revealed. Béguin sees Nodier as an heir to German Romanticism, a Romanticism that stresses the relationship between the dreaming and the waking state of man and which is, in many ways, on a much deeper and more philosophical and psychological level than French Romanticism. But Béguin also warns that one should not attempt to interpret the work too closely and thereby destroy the poetry and the poetic images that the work entails.

Each critic, of course, attempts to interpret *La Fée aux miettes* on the basis of his own disposition, his own affinities, his own erudition and background, as well as on the basis of his own personal problems and hangups; and each critic can, without much difficulty, always discover in the work, the appropriate quotation with which to substantiate his interpretation. With this in mind, it is perhaps interesting to examine briefly two critics who approach this work from points of view that are other than purely esthetic, namely Jules Vodoz and André Lebois.

Jules Vodoz, by using as subtitle "Essai sur le rôle du subconscient dans l'oeuvre de Charles Nodier," indicates immediately that he is attempting to examine Nodier's work from a psychoanalytical point of view, thereby attempting to interpret Nodier's life, his loves, his most secret desires and needs through his work. The basic premise Vodoz makes in his study is that in *La Fée aux miettes* we detect a subconscious expression of guilt: guilt for the love Nodier felt for his daughter. Vodoz then proceeds to see in the main characters symbolical meanings. Nodier is Michel, Vodoz tells us; which is, of course, quite true. Nodier, as we have seen, projected himself in almost all of his characters. And Michel is no exception. In his preface to *La Fée aux miettes*, Nodier declares joyfully that he resembles Michel, only "a little less mad." But the symbolical significances do not stop there. According to Vodoz, Michel and, by extension, Nodier, has a number of additional alter egos. One alter ego is Michel's companion for the night, Sir Jap, the bailiff with the head of a Great Dane. Sir Jap, says Vodoz, represents the second nature, the sensual and material nature of Michel/Nodier. "To pull the blanket over his companion and himself implies that he is identifying with his double, the dog, the beast." [39] This second "I," which is accepted and, at the same time, repudiated by Michel, is, nevertheless, a very appealing second nature; the bailiff is, after all, a very honorable and pleasant dinner and bed companion. Vodoz sees a third alter ego in the character of the Jew, Jonathas, symbolizing a baser, material nature and who withdraws after Michel's moral victory. Maître Finewood is still a fourth alter ego. Vodoz sees evidence for this analogy between Nodier and Maître Finewood in the fact that the master carpenter eventually permits his six daughters to marry poor, but honest, young men instead of the six noblemen. Vodoz sees a correlation between this and Nodier's final acceptance of his daughter's marriage to Jules Mennessier. In Maître Finewood, Nodier "recognizes his rational 'self,' his good sense, his practical sense." [40] In the end, continues Vodoz, "Michel, Maître Finewood and Nodier merge together to become one." [41]

Vodoz also sees in the character of the Fée aux Miettes the mother neither Michel nor Nodier ever had, adding that she also stands for the mother Nodier never cared to know. Later in the study, Vodoz states that the Fée aux Miettes represents Nodier's wife, Désirée, and that Belkiss is his daughter, Marie "the mother become younger," [42] which may, of course, be quite accurate but not very significant. That fathers often see in their daughters a portrait of a younger wife is quite common. Nevertheless, one wonders to what extent such an explanation enhances the comprehension and enjoyment of the work itself. Vodoz also sees another analogy in the relationship between Michel and Folly Girlfree. According to Vodoz, in his meeting with Folly Girlfree, Michel acquires another "self," another identity, which happens to coincide with the identity that Nodier acquired with the birth of his daughter, for Folly Girlfree also symbolizes his daughter, a daughter who tempts him but whom he resists. Indeed, in the tale Michel, who is facing death for the murder of Sir Jap, is told by his judges that he can go free if he can find a girl who will love and marry him. Folly Girlfree is that girl and offers herself. But to choose Folly Girlfree means to be unfaithful to the Fée aux Miettes and this he refuses to do even though it means his death.

Thus, once more, Michel successfully passes the test that has been imposed upon him and he comes a step closer to attaining the ideal. Vodoz sees here an analogy between Michel's salvation and that of Nodier. Nodier's spiritual self has vanquished his material self; he has not fallen into temptation.

The second approach is that of André Lebois, which he presents in his essay *Un Bréviaire du compagnonnage: La Fée aux Miettes de Charles Nodier*. According to Lebois, *La Fée aux miettes* is not merely a fairy tale for adults; rather, it is a fairy tale for adult education and places the stress on the word "education." As the title of Lebois' essay implies, *La Fée aux miettes* is a breviary for the teaching of the ethical principles and the secret codes and rituals of the Brotherhood of the Freemasons. It is written, says Lebois, for the edification of all those humble and simple workers who were confused by the revolution of 1830, by the struggle of the classes, and the fallacious programmes that were organized at the time. Lebois feels that the tale should be examined in the context of such essays as *De la perfectibilité de l'homme, De la Fin prochaine du genre humain,* and *De l'Utilité morale de l'instruction pour le peuple,* all written in 1830 and 1831. To these one should perhaps add Nodier's essay entitled *De la Maçonnerie et du Carbonarisme* (1833). Furthermore, says Lebois, *La Fée aux miettes* should not be considered as a novel but, rather, as an allegory. The key to an understanding of this allegory lies in the sentence: "It is the handsome carpenter of Granville who is engaged to the widow of Salomon." Salomon, Lebois explains, is closely involved in Masonic legends. Likewise is Saint Michel, "prince of created light." And, adds Lebois, the setting of Mont-Saint-Michel is symbolical of the Pyramid, which is a Masonic emblem, as is the importance of the feast of Saint Michel; equally important is the naming of the hero, Michel. The characters, too, must be taken allegorically. The Fée aux Miettes is the "Mère des Compagnons," giving practical advice to one and all. Michel is the "compagnon parfait" of the Brotherhood, the Brother who adheres diligently and faithfully to the teachings of Freemasonry: virtue, humility, industry, patience, faith, love, and charity. And the tests which Michel undergoes are the tests that the initiate has to undergo before he can be accepted into the Brotherhood.

## V   L'Histoire d'Hélène Gillet (*1832*)

*L'Histoire d'Hélène Gillet* is one of Nodier's most brutal and most compassionate tales. According to Nodier, it is based upon an historical event; it is also reminiscent of an incident that occurred in 1820 when Monique Saquel was accused of infanticide. Her guilt was never really established, and Nodier, as did many other writers, intervened on her behalf. Nodier fears that the tale he is to tell will revolt the reader's delicate sensibilities and claims that he, himself, had difficulty writing the story, so repugnant was it. Indeed, the beginning of the tale is somewhat reminiscent of the gothic novel, *The Monk,* by Matthew G. Lewis, where the monk, Ambrosio, rapes the sweet and innocent Antonia. When we first meet Hélène we are informed that she has been drugged and raped by "one of these violent type of men who sacrifice everything to their passions, including the woman who is the object of their passion." [43] Having once been beautiful, pure, virtuous, rich, and, therefore, envied, Hélène, after her downfall, becomes the object of much scorn and brutality, even on the part of her own father. She gives birth to a child and immediately falls into a long coma. A young man enters her room, places a kiss on her forehead, and steals the newly born infant. It is assumed that it is the same individual who had raped her in the first place, and we suspect the young tutor of her brothers. Finally Hélène wakes up and Nodier's description of this moment is rather touching.

When Hélène woke up and realized the full extent of her misery, she probably looked for her child; it was no longer there. She dared not ask for it, for it seemed to her that she should not have had a child. And all these events piled up in her mind like the caprices of a vision.[44]

Later, the dead child is discovered buried outside the city walls. Hélène is accused of murder, tried and condemned "to be beheaded, for we know that Hélène was of noble blood and it was then believed that steel ennobled agony. Since that time steel has become more popular." [45] The practice of cutting off heads in 1624, the date of the action, did, indeed, become more popular during the revolution as Nodier is implying here.

Much of the tale is devoted to the actual attempt to execute Hélène, which turns out to be a somewhat difficult proposition, and portrays, with disgust and irony, the bloodthirsty crowd as it watches and clamors for the execution. The executioner, Simon Grandjean, is, on the other hand, portrayed sympathetically, and his pity for the young girl is pathetic and touching. Weakened by fasting and an illness, Grandjean pleads to be excused from having to kill Hélène. "I have never severed any heads," he says, "and our Lord is denying me the strength to kill this young girl! . . . Upon my faith as a Christian, I know that I cannot kill her." [46] But the crowd howls with fury at the thought of being deprived of blood and gore, and cries out: "Kill! Kill!" And the procurator of the king says solemnly and dutifully to the executioner: "Do your duty." [47] So Grandjean takes the cutlass and, stumbling, falls at her feet and begs Hélène to forgive him and asks her to kill him instead. And Hélène quietly answers: "I forgive you and bless you." [48] and places her head on the block. Grandjean, pushed by his wife (being an executioner is a family affair), strikes at Hélène, but misses. He strikes again and misses a second time. He does, however, manage to hit her shoulder with the cutlass and she falls down. At this point the mood of the mob changes; its fury and impatience turns in favor of Hélène and against Grandjean. Thus Grandjean, the one man kindly disposed to Hélène, is killed by the angry mob, aided by the venerable guild of masons who had also turned out to watch the execution. Furthermore, "the guild of butchers organized itself behind the guild of masons as a reserve corps, all ready for the murder." [49] But that is not the end. There is more to come. The executioner's wife, determined to do her duty—after all, had not the procurator of the king told her husband to do his duty—searches for the cutlass. Unable to find it—Hélène is lying on it—she takes her scissors and stabs Hélène several times. She then drags Hélène down the steps, letting her head bump as it hits each step. As she reaches the bottom step, the butchers "had completed their first job." [50] Now it was time for the mob to get into the act: together with the butchers, they kill the executioner's wife.

What is so startling about this tale is the matter-of-factness with which Nodier tells the story. It is as though the subject matter were so horrible that Nodier had to appear as distant as possible to prevent himself from being too moved. Indeed, when one compares this work with *La Fée aux miettes* or *Trilby*, one suddenly becomes aware that the writer is not at all present; this is felt, despite (and perhaps because of) the fact that Nodier frequently speaks directly to the reader. His attitude is made clear when, in reference to the tale, he says: "This is, unfortunately, neither poetry nor a novel; it is, alas, only history." [51] Yet, when one compares Nodier's account of the event with the original account given in a long footnote, one becomes aware that this tale is, indeed, more than the recounting of an historical event and that the author's own poetic vision is very much present. This is especially apparent in the portrayal of the old nun, Françoise du Saint-Esprit, who had predicted that Hélène would not die by the hand of an executioner. Furthermore, Simon Grandjean, unlike the executioner in the historical account, becomes an individual. These human and personal qualities are enhanced through the use of dialogue which gives the tale its dramatic quality.

## VI  *Capital Punishment*

Throughout much of his work, and especially in *L'Histoire d'Hélène Gillet,* Nodier makes frequent ironic remarks about judges, justice, executioners, whom he calls "legal assassins," and capital punishment. There is an ironic touch when Nodier juxtaposes the execution of Hélène with the marriage ceremony of Charles I of England. A similar juxtaposition is made at the end of the tale when, twenty-four years later, it is the head of Charles I that is falling at Whitehall "with an axe that is more assured than that of Simon Grandjean." [52] But Hélène, unlike the unconcerned Monarch on his wedding day, prays for the monarch's salvation.

In an unprecedented manner, Nodier tells the reader that there is a moral to this story. In a scathing attack against the institution of legalized murder, Nodier says:

It would be high time for mankind to reject with an unanimous voice this blasphemous justice which insolently usurped God's power to mete out death—this power that God kept for himself when he struck our entire race with a death sentence on his very own. Oh! you are great makers of revolution! You have made revolutions against all the moral and political institutions of your society! You have made revolutions against all laws! You have made them against the most intimate thoughts of the soul, its affections, its beliefs, its faith! You have made them against thrones, altars, monuments, stones, inanimate objects, death itself, the tomb and the dust of your ancestors! But you did not foster revolutions against the scaffold, for you have never let any human feeling prevail, nor any human emotion palpitate, in your revolution of savages! And you dare speak of your enlightenment! And you do not dread to show yourselves as models of a perfect civilization! Do I dare ask you where it can be found, this civilization of yours? Could it possibly be that hideous vampire sharpening a steel triangle with which to sever heads? Come, you are nothing but barbarians! [53]

And Nodier ends the tale with an impassioned plea to end this kind of killing: "One must not kill anybody. Those who kill must not be killed. The executioner must not be killed. It is the homicidal laws that are to be killed! . . ." [54]

This impassioned plea on the part of Nodier is, indeed, rather unusual, for much of the time he is ironic, expressing his dislike for men who are impressed with their own importance, be they men of law, of science, or of the cloth—who, alas, form the majority of the leaders of mankind. In his *Epilogue* of *Souvenirs et Portraits de la Révolution,* Nodier says that affairs of state are usually "abandoned to puppets in silk stockings and red heels or to pedants in a black gown and square bonnet." [55] We see his contempt for laws because most laws are made by men who are stupid and who have no feeling for humanity. In *L'Histoire d'Hélène Gillet* we see before us a man who is ashamed to belong to the human race because he feels all the barbarous actions of men and all the barbarity that is tied to the institution of capital punishment; he feels its cowardice and its hypocrisy because he knows that more innocent than guilty men have been the victims of the executioner's blade. The spectacle of injustice horrifies him as does the spectacle of man's inhumanity to man as the mob screams for vengeance and for blood.

Justice, beheadings, and capital punishment all greatly preoccupied Nodier and contributed very markedly to making the world an unpleasant place for him. His contacts with the legal system were considerable, for his father was president of the "Tribunal Criminel" of Doubs during the revolution, which undoubtedly afforded Nodier close contact with the world of justice and crime and courts. Inevitably, the gruesome spectacle of executions left a strong impression upon the mind of a sensitive youth and explains his obsessions with severed, rolling, and bloody heads. Although an execution is most explicit in *L'Histoire d'Hélène Gillet,* a brief but gruesome description of an execution is also evident in *Smarra* and in *La Fée aux miettes.* In *Smarra* the dreamer-narrator expresses the gruesome experience of his own execution:

More serene now, I relinquished my head to the intensely keen and icy sword of the death officer. Never had a more penetrating shudder run between a man's vertebrae; it was as startling as the last kiss imprinted by fever on the neck of a moribund, as sharp as tempered steel, as consuming as molten lead. My only relief from this anguish came by way of a terrible commotion: my head had fallen off . . . rolling down and bouncing on the hideous floor of the scaffold and ready to drop down, all bruised, into the hands of the children—Larissa's lovely children who play with the heads of dead men—it had attached itself to a jutting board by biting into it with those iron jaws that rage lends to agonizing men. From there, I let my glance fall on the crowd that was now leaving, silent, but satisfied. . . .

I was biting obstinately, the humid wood, wet with my recently spilled blood . . .[56]

In *La Fée aux miettes*, it will be recalled, Michel was accused of having murdered the bailiff, Sir Jap. For this supposed crime, Michel is tried and sentenced to death amid the enthusiastic clamor of the crowds who, like the crowds of other executions, were "panting with impatience and voluptuousness," [57] crying out "there he is" when they saw the victim. Here, too, Nodier refers to executions as "legal butcheries" [58] maintained by a civilization that is still at the level of "cannibalism." But Michel feels nothing but pity and contempt for the crowd:

I diverted my glance from [the scaffold] not from terror, for I craved death as much as one craves to be awakened from a painful dream, but from a mixture of pity and disgust of which I became aware only after a while. One cannot begin to understand what contempt or what compassion for mankind fills the heart of an innocent man who is about to die.[59]

And in an essay entitled *Souvenirs et Portraits de la Révolution*, Nodier says that "a nation which considers murder as just, legal, and heroic, has nothing that places it above the level of cannibals." [60] In this same work he devotes several pages to his friend and tutor, the Abbé Euloge Schneider, whom he had met in Strasbourg and who also succumbed to the terror in Alsace and whose execution he describes in this work.

VII   Le Songe d'or (*1832*), Jean-François les Bas-Bleus (*1832*)
   *and* Baptiste Montauban ou l'idiot (*1833*)

The terms "innocent" and "voyant" are also applicable to such characters as Xaïloun, the woodcutter and village idiot, Jean-François, who became a lunatic through the acquisition of too much knowledge, and Baptiste Montauban, who possesses the power of divination and who dies from a broken heart. They, too, occupy in Nodier's work the highest rung of the ladder, although in the real world they are the creatures who are scorned and ridiculed by those who run society and dictate its customs and mores; that is, those who are insensitive, crude, aggressive, and greedy.

The theme of *Le Songe d'or* centers around a treasure and six characters from this world and one from the other world. Each creature reacts to the treasure according to his condition and disposition. The first creature to discover the treasure hidden in the desert is a lizard, a *kardouon*. He goes up to it, pleased, because he thinks it is food and is happy at the thought of being able to share it with other lizards. He takes the treasure, places it in a damp cold place, tries a nice tempting golden nugget and promptly breaks a tooth. "It's old and dry," the lizard remarks and, tired, goes to sleep. Soon the woodcutter Xaïloun, "one of those children ill-treated by nature," [61] the village idiot whom everybody mocks, approaches the treasure. In his loneliness Xaïloun had sought out the *kardouon* who, himself timid, had run away. In his despair and sorrow Xaïloun ran away from home. But as he comes upon the treasure and the *kardouon* in the desert, Xaïloun has eyes only for the *kardouon,* for what does an innocent one want with gold and riches? Since the evening is cool, he takes off his coat and spreads it over the lizard. He then lies near his friend and dreams of the joys of friendship. Soon a fakir comes along, a man who has vowed to live in poverty and work for the wonder of God. When he sees the treasure he immediately believes that it is a sign from God, a recompense for years of devout service to God. But the evening is cold, and his lids become heavy. Soon he, too, falls asleep. He is soon followed by a doctor of law, a learned man who yearns for riches and power. He, too, sees the treasure and in the legal jargon of lawyers, he pleads his case. Nodier is now the "dériseur sensé" who satirizes pedants,

cads, academicians, quacks, etc. Sleep soon overcomes him. While
traveling through the desert, the lawyer had been closely followed
by a brigand, the King of the Sand-dunes. When the latter arrives
on the scene, he right away wants to kill all the sleepers and run
off with the treasure. But he, too, succumbs to sleep and prefers to
await the morning. He dreams of murder, plunder, and lizards
roasting on charcoal.

Finally the sage Lochman appears, who is also a poet. It is becoming morning by now. Since he is old, it had taken Lochman a
great deal of time to cover distances. He sees the treasure and all
the sleeping creatures. He analyzes the scene and understands the
workings of the minds of men and *kardouons*. "And," he adds, "all
five went to sleep in the poisoned shadow of an upas tree." [62] Indeed, all are dead, poisoned by the tree, and Lochman buries
them all nearby. But he buries Xaïloun and the *kardouon* together, for he knows that Xaïloun loved the *kardouon*. He also
buries the treasure, hoping thereby to save a man or a lizard from
its dreadful clutches. He then returns to the place where he had
buried Xaïloun and the *kardouon*, lies down next to them, and
dies.

The next day an angel of God with great blue wings comes
down to earth to fetch Xaïloun "whom heaven awaits, because he
is innocent and simple of heart." [63] He also discovers Lochman,
poet and sage, equally the beloved of God. Receiving from the
angel the kiss of resurrection, Lochman goes to heaven to live in
eternal bliss with God. And, adds Nodier, the story of these seven
characters is also the story of the world.

Jean-François, like Xaïloun, is the laughingstock of his town.
Son of a tailor who had spared nothing to give his son a good
education in the hope that he would become a priest and whose
outstanding sermons would make him a bishop, he is now all the
more scorned because his education had come to naught. Indeed,
for a while, he had been an excellent pupil and had been the
apple of the teacher's eye. But soon matters changed. Jean-
François paid little attention to worldly matters; his eyes were
eternally fixed heavenward and his lips moved incessantly, mut-
tering words known only to himself and to his maker. He was
considered mad because whenever one talked to him about familiar, mundane things, about the weather, the theater, items in the
newspaper, the latest gossip, he would listen politely but his re-

plies would be sheer babbling and his logic was far from Cartesian or Aristotelian. However, if one talked to him about ethical and scientific problems, such as the nature of the material and spiritual world, the coexistence of these two worlds, or the nature of knowledge, Jean-François would demonstrate a keen sense of understanding and appreciation and give answers that revealed true wisdom. It was difficult for the narrator to try to reconcile these two aspects of Jean-François, and he attempted to explain this seeming paradox by giving to him two different souls: one which belonged to the material world in which we lived, and one which shed its material self and entered into the world of pure thought.[64] It was obvious that this distinction could be appreciated only by minds of equal stature, sensitive to the intricacies of a complex and imaginative mind. But matters are further aggravated when Jean-François predicts the execution of Marie-Antoinette and which only the narrator takes seriously.

Baptiste Montauban, another innocent and idiot, solitary and inoffensive, is pushed into his condition because he loved honestly. As a child he had caught the attention of his father's boss, Monsieur Dubourg, who had pitied his poverty and admired his intelligence. Unfortunately, Baptiste falls in love with Dubourg's daughter, Rosette. But Monsieur Dubourg has other plans for his daughter, and Baptiste is sent back to his mother. Although he tries to distract himself with his studies, with nature, he cannot forget her. He isolates himself more and more from the society of men; animals, birds, and trees are now his sole companions. He spends all his time talking to them; the birds even allow him to catch them because they know he will do them no harm. But the children of the town—those children whose imagination and innocence have already been damaged by society—want him to give them the birds, which he refuses to do after he discovers that they put the birds in cages, mutilate them, and even eat them. Baptiste, like Jean-François and Xaïloun, dies, and his soul, freed of its material self, enters the world of pure being.

These three tales, especially *Jean-François les Bas-Bleus* and *Baptiste Montauban,* are very similar to *Une Heure ou la Vision* and *La Filleule du Seigneur* of the Wertherian cycle. To some degree we will meet them once again when Nodier writes his mystical tales.

We have seen that in the tales belonging to the cycle of the *voyants* and the innocents, the dream, nocturnal and diurnal, and the fantastic and the marvelous, play a dominant role. It is primarily in these tales that the line of demarcation between reality and the dream grows dim and the two worlds begin to fuse. In this world live individuals who are outside the pale of everyday existence and whose imagination and ability to create worlds of their own make them incomprehensible to the solid and prosaic citizens. They are the lunatics, the pure and simple of heart, those creatures endowed with a sixth sense because they have not been contaminated by the "real" world, the world of progress, science, technology, and positivism. Nonetheless, these works, as we have seen, also contain elements that belong to the cycle of the "dériseur sensé." This is especially true of *L'Histoire d'Hélène Gillet* where criticism of society and its institutions come under rigorous attack.

# CHAPTER 6

# The Cycle of the "Dériseur Sensé"

ALONG with the cycle of the *voyants* and the innocents and covering approximately the same period, we discern another cycle which both Castex and Jean Richer have called the cycle of the "dériseur sensé," that is, the cycle of the sensible and judicious mocker. It is in this cycle that the theme of progress and perfectibility is questioned and satirized, although criticism of society and satire also played an important role in such works as *La Fée aux miettes, L'Histoire d'Hélène Gillet, Baptiste Montauban,* and others. Indeed, in these works institutions, the implementation of justice, universal education, and capital punishment, had already been ridiculed; in them Nodier had already expressed the idea that society is composed of "tant de sots" who teach children to lack imagination, as well as "to hate each other, and to read and write, that is, all those things which they lacked, in order to make horrible creatures out of them." [1] However, it is themes such as the dream, innocence, the state of grace, love, and faith, that dominate; the mood and tone are more positive, and there is a quest to undertake and a lesson to be heeded. The very existence of two such parallel cycles coexisting with each other, even complementing each other, indicates that Nodier, the satirist and judicious mocker, needed also Nodier, the builder of dreams and myths, the creator of the magical world of childhood, a world filled with childlike, simple people: the innocents and the dispossessed of the world. It was essential, as Castex puts it, to oppose a cycle of innocence to the cycle of corruption.

To the cycle of the "dériseur sensé" belong such tales as *Hurlubleu, Grand Manifafa d'Hurlubière ou la Perfectibilité* (1833), *Leviathan le Long Archikan des Patagons de l'île savante, ou la Perfectibilité, pour faire suite à Hurlubleu* (1833), *Zerothoctro-Schah, Proto-Mystagogue de Bactriane* (probably written around 1833 but published as late as 1961), and *Voyage pittoresque et*

*industriel dans le Paraguay-Roux et la Palingénésie australe*
(1836), covering a period between 1833 to 1836. Two other works
will be discussed in this context although there are some major
differences: *La plus petite des pantoufles* (1805) and *L'Histoire
du Roi de Bohême et de ses sept châteaux* (1830). A number of
essays written in 1830 and 1831, although they are of a serious
nature, will be discussed here because they, too, deal with such
themes as perfectibility, progress, and universal education. They
are: *De la Perfectibilité de l'homme* (1830), *De la Fin prochaine
du genre humain* (1831), and *De l'Utilité morale de l'instruction
pour le peuple* (1831).

## I   De la Perfectibilité de l'homme (*1830*)

We have, by now, come to realize that Nodier ridicules such
notions as perfectibility and progress[2] and have seen him attack
and ridicule these ideas in many of his works. But in his essay *De
la Perfectibilité de l'homme* Nodier discusses at length his opposition to the idea of perfectibility and explains why he opposes it.
Nodier does not believe in the idea of perfectibility because to do
so assumes that the nature of man can be changed. Nodier can not
and will not believe in any change in man's nature because he
believes that man's basic nature has been constant ever since recorded history. However, Nodier quickly explains that this does
not mean that some sort of global revolution, followed by the creation of a new species, created either intelligently or spontane-
ously, cannot arise in the future. This new species would by no
means be identical with our present species; moreover, this
process would be "creation" rather than "perfectibility" since it
would involve a totally new species. Nodier thus believes in a
branching development of life rather than in a linear development, thereby anticipating Darwin by a number of years. Nonetheless, Nodier admits to some sort of progress and perfectibility,
but only in the domain of technology. This so-called perfectibility,
says Nodier, was achieved through the development of the hand
which made application of ingenious instruments and devices
possible. However, insofar as the speculative or pure sciences are
concerned, Nodier believes that they have not moved ahead very
much; they are by nature unchangeable because nature, itself, is
unchangeable and therefore not perfectible. Even the factual or
applied sciences, although they did, indeed, advance—or, rather,

they increased in knowledge—they, too, are not perfectible. And although man realized new existences, attempted new analyses, and discovered new methods, one cannot really call these phenomena creation or perfectibility. Men of the eighteenth or nineteenth century may have considered themselves the discoverers of new inventions and new ideas, but, because of their ignorance of history and past achievements, they thought they had discovered something new and unique. For example, inventions such as printing, printer's ink, playing cards, and rag paper are really nothing new; they can be traced back to the ancient Greeks, Egyptians, and Chinese. In the final analysis, says Nodier, "from Christopher Columbus to Punchinello, whose grotesque type was discovered in Egyptian statuettes as old as the Pyramids, we have not progressed one step on any scientific ground that had not already been touched upon by previous generations." [3] Thus, insists Nodier, notions such as perfectibility, progress, and the millennium, are nothing but illusions which derive from man's vain and ambitious nature, which believes that our species, man, like the individual, is immortal. The only things man can be sure of are birth and death. Man "is born, he grows, lives, and ages, embracing more and more of a future that he cannot truly reach; then he dies without ever having attained any part of what he had desired. The story of the individual is the story of nations." [4] Equally responsible for man's illusions is his desire for absolute truth. In an essay entitled *Qu'est-ce que la vérité?* Nodier discusses the impossibility of ever securing truth. "The need for absolute truth," Nodier says, "is instinctive in our species; the impossibility of attaining it is its misery." [5] Because man dies and is unhappy he goes in search of certainty, the absolute, and the ideal, be it in the form of a mandrake that sings, the blue flower of Novalis or Musset, the black tulip of Baudelaire, or the Holy Grail of Parsifal.

## II   De la Fin prochaine du genre humain (*1831*)

In his article entitled *De la Fin prochaine du genre humain,* Nodier goes beyond the idea of denying man his perfectibility; in this essay he believes that the human species is on the decline and will soon become extinct. Man, in his desire for perfectibility, in his yearning for the amelioration of the species, has completely ignored the possibility of the extinction of the species. After all, says Nodier, everything in the universe evolves and dies; everything passes from the simple to the complex and back again to the simple. Man, as an individual, evolves and dies and, by analogy, so does the species man—it, too, must evolve and die. An existence that is considered complete, that is, that has reached its apogee, is an existence that is on the decline and will soon reach its end. "All species end," Nodier reminds us, "thus the species *man* must end." [6] Nature will then produce other species which, in turn, will develop and eventually disappear. Immortality belongs only to nature; it, alone, is eternal. Furthermore, adds Nodier, making a statement that sounds prophetic, "bodies that are organically the most simple are also the most durable." [7] Civilizations, likewise, experience cycles and undergo similar processes. It is in the nature of civilizations to go through the cycles of development and decline. After civilizations have reached their apogee and have become too complex, decline is inevitable; irreparable infirmities, excessive passions and vices bring about a return to the state of barbarism or to total annihilation. Wars, revolutions, and invasions precipitate—though they do not necessarily cause—this return to barbarism. The barbarism of today will differ from the barbarism of the past in that the barbarism man is presently experiencing has begun under the slogan of progress and perfectibility, thus fooling people about the true state of things.

### III   De l'Utilité morale et de l'instruction pour le peuple ( *1831* )

The third essay dealing with the decline of man and his impending doom is *De l'Utilité morale et de l'instruction pour le peuple*. In this essay Nodier questions the utility of education, above all, universal education. In the year 1750, the Academy of Dijon had proposed the following question: "Has the restoration of the sciences and the arts tended to purify morals?" We all know that a certain citizen of Geneva, by the name of Jean-Jacques Rousseau, answered this question with a resounding "No." In the opinion of Nodier, the Academy of Dijon should have asked the question in the following manner: "What is the utility of instruction and what benefits did civilization reap through the invention of writing?" [8] We thus find Nodier agreeing with Rousseau in his

belief that progress has corrupted man and that education does
not benefit him whatsoever. The school of nature alone can teach
man, concludes Nodier. To try to remedy the situation, Nodier
urges that society give back to the nation "its oral instruction, its
memories, its traditions. . . . Let this generation which reads,
writes, and counts, come to an end, and do not talk to us about it
any more." [9]

## IV   Reading the Classics

It should perhaps be pointed out that Nodier is not totally negative in his ideas on education and that he does, indeed, make
some positive suggestions with respect to the education of the
young. These suggestions, however, are scattered here and there
in his tales. Although Nodier condemns "l'enseignement mutuel et
la méthode Jacotot," [10] a sort of universal education conceived by
Jacotot during the early part of the nineteenth century, and many
of the books given to children and adults, he by no means condemns all learning and all books. Homer's *Odyssey* is one of the
books Nodier cherishes above all others and recommends for children and adults alike. The *Odyssey* is a great and sublime work
Nodier says in *Paul ou la ressemblance*, because in it we discern
the existence of faith, innocence, and imagination; above all, there
is, on the part of the author, a belief in what he is saying. These
are the very traits, says Nodier, that modern man no longer possesses; and learning, scientific discoveries, and technology have
done much to destroy these very qualities in the *Odyssey*. What a
terrible tragedy it is, for us as well as for Homer, suddenly to
realize that the sirens Homer described were perhaps nothing
more than seals or sea cows. Other books that contribute to man's
happiness and moral instruction and develop the imaginative faculty are

those delightful creations which capture the soul with such lively sym-
pathies and which permeate it with so useful and sweet a knowledge:
the *Odyssey, The Voyages of Pinto, Perrault's Contes*, the *Fables of
Pilpay, Aesop*, and *La Fontaine, Telemachus, Robinson, Don Quixote,
The Flying Men!* One realizes clearly that in these books the emotions
of men are the main concern; but what books and what men, Good
Lord, are those I have just named! Here is money well spent! Here is a
library of genuine *humanitarian progress! . . .* [11]

It is evident that when Nodier is criticizing society and culture, he is criticizing a society and a culture that is advancing scientifically and technologically but whose progress is not accompanied by the development of "humanitarian progress" or a "moral conscience." Thus, Nodier stands for progress and education that develops the moral nature of man, his sense of happiness and, above all, his imagination, his ability to dream and create new worlds; education must be devoid of pedantry, dogmatism, quackery, and pomposity. He is against a society that surrenders itself to a handful of pedants and cads and inept medical men whose only skill is the use of their special jargon and quack remedies such as curing lunatics with spinning chairs and other such "progressive" techniques and notions.

## V La plus petite des pantoufles (1805)

Although written as early as 1805, this little work has been placed with the tales and essays that belong to the cycle of the "dériseur sensé" for the following reasons: it is an early and much shorter version of *Le Roi de Bohême et de ses sept châteaux* (this 1805 version had, in turn, an even earlier draft which goes back to 1800, entitled *Le Prince Bibi;* Bibi is also the protagonist of the 1805 tale); furthermore, like *Le Roi de Bohême*, this tale is imbued with a certain lightness and frivolity, a mock-serious tone, and attempts to satirize learning, pedants, savants, tyrants, and the like. Any attempt to give an exact analysis of the subject matter can only fail, since *La plus petite des pantoufles* is a pastiche that is as elusive as it is charming. It has the flavor of a fairy tale; but it is not a fairy tale in the traditional manner with a narrative that, in true Aristotelian fashion, has a beginning, a middle, and an end. It starts in the middle of things, and its subtitles mystify rather than enlighten one. Quite obviously, one must not take this little tale seriously as Nodier is very quick to make clear at the very outset when he tells us that the tale occurred "many moons before the discovery of elastic garters." [12] It is in this context that we meet King Bibi who, without much ado, promptly loses his wife and his hackney. Whereupon King Bibi immediately sets out to seek the Fée des Pantoufles who has her domain in the ear of the Big Bear. She then sends him off on a quest (it is, indeed, reminiscent of *La Fée aux miettes*) to the land of the Galimathias on Pathos, the capital of the great kingdom of Baliverne where

King Bibi will meet all the great savants who are endowed with
the ability to reason excellently on every subject and who can
immediately tell the difference between weak and strong reasoning. In the meantime King Bibi gets a one-eyed mare. Together
they set out for the metropolis of Galimathias. But before they
reach the city, Nodier, in true Rabelaisian fashion, demonstrates
that learning is something very serious; we are also informed that
this work is intended to be a "compendium of all the sciences." [13]
In the process, we are given a brief summary of the various fields
of learning and the names of some philosophers. It took Bibi and
the mare seven days to cross Galimathias. This is what happened
on their trip:

> On the first day everybody cried.
> On the second day everybody laughed.
> On the third day everybody made a face.
> On the fourth day everybody walked on the double.
> On the fifth day everybody went on all fours.
> On the sixth day everybody danced the "Montferrin."
> On the seventh day everybody fought over the word
>     that belonged to an enigma.

But when everybody noticed that his mare was one-eyed, they
gathered behind him and followed him to his hotel, where one counted
thirteen thousand eleven people who cried out as loudly as possible:
"His mare is one-eyed! His mare is one-eyed! And of all of the one-
eyed mares this one is the most one-eyed." [14]

There is something preposterous and absurd about the image
we get of a king, a one-eyed mare and a group of people doing
basically normal things but which, given their juxtaposition, express a nonsensical and absurd condition. It is, indeed, the absurd
world of childhood; but it is also the absurd world of the dream
filled with oneiric puns, allusions, and images that emerge from
the deep recesses of the unconscious mind. As such, Nodier can be
considered a precursor of Pataphysics, which is "the science of
imaginary solutions." [15] Not only does Nodier anticipate Alfred
Jarry's *Gestes et Opinions du Docteur Faustroll*, but in this work
he also anticipates the Benjamin Péret of *Main Forte* or *Une
Brebis galante* with his attempt to reproduce the dream and the
automatic writing that is to emerge from a dream or trance. This
is especially true of the scene when King Bibi is obliged to attend

the reading of a five-act play. Both he and the mare are bored, and King Bibi is especially worried about the mare's welfare.

We played hot-water bottle, blindman's buff, and wet finger. We drank Vermoute and Mirobolanti. Bibi went out without being noticed, and I believe he was very pleased.

REPARATION

"Forgive me, Madam," said the King to his mare.

—I did not get bored, Sire, she answered. I spent the time talking to an Andalousian bay who complained about being mounted and carried by Olive and of having to serve as a carriage horse as well as a saddle horse to a countess who bleached her silk stockings.

—And did this Andalousian bay wear silk stockings? asked the King.

—Indeed, Sire, said the mare, "when the stocks fell." [16]

### VI   Le Roi de Bohême et de ses sept châteaux ( 1830 )

Nodier's *Roi de Bohême* is even more difficult to place and more elusive to analyze than *La plus petite des pantofles*. It is a mosaic of many themes, authors, and styles. It is a satire, for Nodier is making fun of the institutions, ideas, and ideals of a mythical kingdom, Timbuctoo, its academy and academics, and its autocratic king; it is a metaphysical and allegorical work in that the characters represent abstract ideas, in this case, the "mysterious trinity of our intelligence," [17] imagination, memory, and judgment, and includes his favorite theme: dream and reality. It is a pastiche, as Nodier himself points out, "of the numerous pastiches of Sterne and Rabelais." [18] But it is also an imitation of a host of other authors: Cervantes, Cyrano de Bergerac, Swift, Montaigne, Marot, and Amyot; practically all the writers he loved so well are represented. Like *La plus petite des pantoufles*, this work is subdivided into irregular chapters that bear such strangely reminiscent titles as "Objection," "Déclaration," "Protestation," "Damnation," "Aberration," "Mystification," "Méditation," "Navigation," "Exhumation." The *Roi de Bohême* also concerns itself with language, playing with words and sounds, juxtaposing images, as though he knew about the Symbolists and Surrealists. Similar to its antecedent, the *Roi de Bohême* has adopted a spoofing, mock-serious tone with an equally licentious undertone; but unlike *La plus petite des pantoufles*, it spends a considerable amount of time analyzing and synthesizing the meaning and origin of the word "pantoufle." The work resembles its early predecessor in that it, too, starts out with a discussion of a hackney, Lénore, and, toward the end, we come across a mare called Patricia—but one is not quite sure whether we are dealing with a horse or a woman, and the confusion leads to erotic suggestions. But, then, knowing Nodier, the entire work may well be nothing more than a long, extended dream, with all the inconsistencies, digressions, absurdities that are inherent in dreams, especially if the dreamer has a vivid imagination.

And what, asks Nodier, is the aim of such a book as this? Nothing, really. What, after all, is the aim of a dream? But Nodier tries to be helpful. "In our age," he says, "the most pressing need for a reasonable man who appreciates the world and life on its own terms, is to know the end of the story of the King of Bohemia and his seven castles." [19] Eventually, after all sorts of detours, which give him the chance to describe places or tell stories, the narrator arrives at his first castle in Koeniggratz, "the saddest of the seven castles of Bohemia." [20]

Loosely stated, the book centers around the narrator Théodore/Nodier, King of Bohemia, who wants to visit his seven castles somewhere near Spain. Only he does not want to go alone —in fact, he cannot go without Don Pic de Fanferluchio and Breloque, for he is too timid and too innocent. And how will he get there? This becomes a pressing question. By horse and carriage? But does he really need them? Does a sheer stretch of the imagination not permit him to travel more easily and without encountering the usual dangers? And this special carriage of the mind, is it not always ready to take him at any time anywhere he wants to go? "All I have to do," says the narrator, "is snap my fingers or click my tongue three times . . . and. . . ." [21] Besides, the trip is even better with the aid of some crushed betel leaves, a glass of wine, or some of that intoxicating powder he has in his pretty little snuff box. But Nodier is helpful once again. In a letter to his friend Jean de Bry dated December 19, 1829, Nodier is quite explicit as to the nature and aim of the book:

It is a series of reveries, or *"aegrisomnia,"* in which I lose myself in three characters, that is to say, in the three main characters that every educated man can discern in that phenomenon, intelligence: imagination, memory, and judgment. In my case, this ill-assorted trinity is composed of a madman, bizarre and capricious, a pedant well oiled in erudition and nomenclatures, and an honest chap who is rather feeble but sensible and whose impressions are always modified by one or the other of the two. This metaphysical idea is certainly the best one, if not the only one, in the book, but it is so poorly presented, so confused and lost in such an irregular canvas, that I hasten to be the first one to say so.[22]

The work is, indeed, a pastiche of many authors and styles; but above all, it is Rabelais and Sterne who are the guiding lights. The spirit of Rabelais is evident on almost every page; equally prominent is Rabelais' erudition, his love for words, their meanings as well as their sounds. Nodier becomes so imbued with the gigantism and creativeness of Rabelais that he has even become Rabelais. "Rabelais," says Nodier in an essay entitled *Des Types en littérature,* "is the inventor of the most fecund *types* ever created. Every one has gathered what he has reaped. It is brother John, Panurge, Raminagrobis . . . characters . . . whom Rabelais alone has forged." [23] Interestingly enough, Nodier's other guiding light, Laurence Sterne, has, by his own admission, also assumed Rabelais as model. All three do, indeed, have a style that is filled with digressions, ramblings, parodies, portraits, dialogues, intermingled with the greatest extravagances and absurdities; all three take a mock-serious tone and thus attack all the hallowed institutions man has developed throughout the ages. To these traits are added much wit, irony, humor, and learning. These works resemble the intricacies of a patchwork quilt, made up of individual parts which, nevertheless, have a unity and a totality that become obvious after careful consideration and reading. It is precisely this type of literature, a literature which embodies wit and irony, a fine sensibility and a keen sense of observation and erudition but without being pompous about this erudition, that Nodier greatly admires; furthermore, this type of literature also possesses an innocent earthiness about sex and the natural functions of the body, the ability and courage to digress and be extravagant, and to be moral without forcing morality upon one's readers. Nodier found these traits in Rabelais and Sterne; but he found them lacking in much of French literature. This lacuna he discusses clearly in *Voyage . . . dans le Paraguay-Roux:*

What we are lacking in France is not the sharp subtlety of the mind which glides over a superficial ridicule with a pertinent cleverness; we have a surplus of this! What is missing, rather, is the penetrating and profound irony which picks at a ridicule and digs around it (and will not stop shaking it by the roots until it is finally uprooted). Look at Cervantes, look at Butler, look at Swift, look at Sterne: those people do not content themselves with the trimming of *luxuriem foliorum;* they deplete the tree and throw it dead on the ground, deprived of either seeds or shoots. That kind of criticism—which Voltaire and Beaumarchais used to excess, applying it as they did, either with carelessness or malice, to all our remaining social ideas—had models in France, unfortunately difficult to imitate, in Molière and Rabelais; and I must admit, to the prejudice of my own philosophical views, that if literature had its final causes, as all things do, Rabelais and Molière did not appear at the proper time or else, the God of truth is saving for us a Rabelais and a Molière who are greatly delayed in their arrival. . . . What will then be noted as most characteristic of our time is the almost total absence of the *"dériseur sensé"* who has the wit to mock others and to protest with a judicious contempt against the ignorance and madness of his contemporaries.[24]

These lines, written in 1836, serve as a sort of testimony of the real spirit of Nodier, a spirit that existed within him already in 1800 when he expressed, on several occasions, his love for Rabelais and Sterne, and which coexisted with the Wertherian type of sentimental novel so dominant at the time.

An example of Nodier's type of wit and irony, and the way he plays with words is apparent in his analysis, description, history, explanation, explication, and synthesis of the word "pantoufle," a procedure he takes indirectly from Rabelais and Sterne, and a symbol he borrows directly from Sterne. Popocambou, autocrat of Timbuctoo, like Empedocles before him, could think of nothing but his one and only "pantoufle."

He thought of it during the day. He thought of it during the night. He thought of it in the evening. He thought of it in the morning.
He turned on to his left side. He turned on to his right side. He slept on his belly. He slept on his back. He could dream of nothing but his slipper.
It is true that this slipper was not to be scorned. And people would have travelled a long way to meet such a slipper.
It was a thickly lined slipper,
It was a well-padded slipper,
It was a glossy satin slipper,
It was a refined slipper,
It was a perfect slipper,

It was a slipper for the winter, it was a slipper for the summer;
It was an elegant slipper, a svelte slipper, a healthy looking slipper, a
distinguished looking slipper;
It was a well-conditioned slipper, a slipper that was neither too large
nor too narrow, a slipper that was solid, a slipper that had bounce, a
soft slipper, a comfortable slipper, an essential slipper; . . .[25]

It was, indeed, a marvelous slipper, not even behind the times.
In short, it was the queen of slippers. And what about its etymol-
ogy? Well, it may derive from the Greek *"patein"* or *"pholleos"*
which, combined, means "something hollow used for walking." [26]
But why is it in the singular? Because Popocambou was uni-
legged? No, simply because the laws of Timbuctoo stipulated that
while Popocambou was performing his royal functions, he had to
stand at all times on one leg. This is evidence that the reign of
Popocambou was a fertile reign, a reign conducive to progress—
after all, it was he who had the pyramid built. But, in the final
analysis, says Nodier, after much deliberation and rumination,
what difference does it make what the origins of "pantoufle" are.

I would really be mad . . . to get all upset just to know whether
"tophos" or "phellos" went initially into the construction of the name of
a slipper!
    And if I want to be bored this evening . . . is today not the day
when the Bouffes and the Athénée are open? Besides, I added,
                            going
                                down
                                    the
                                        seven
                                            steps
                                                of the
                                                    staircase.
—Besides, Popocambou's sole was not made of cork. It was made of
calf.[27]

According to Jean Richer's essay *Autour de l'Histoire du Roi de
Bohême, Charles Nodier, dériseur sensé,* Nodier is using a *double
entendre,* a sort of oneiric pun, making "pantoufle" stand for a
phallic symbol; this becomes all the more obvious if one is familiar with *Tristram Shandy.* Use of the oneiric pun and the *double
entendre,* and arranging the words on a page so that their very
arrangement gives an added meaning to the words is, of course, a

phenomenon with which we have long since become familiar; one has only to think of Mallarmé, Lewis Carroll, and Apollinaire. Thus, in this domain as well, that is, experimentation with words and form, Nodier goes beyond his masters Rabelais and Sterne and anticipates the Symbolists and the Surrealists.

*Le Roi de Bohême* is also a parody of the Wertherian type of novel that Nodier had once so cherished. What was once a serious attempt to imitate and absorb, in form as well as content, the sentimental epistolary novel, now becomes a parody. The two Wertherian type tales, inserted between the pages of *Le Roi de Bohême* and recounted by the narrator, are *Les Aveugles de Chamouny* and *Histoire du Chien de Brisquet*. To properly understand these two tales, it is of paramount importance that they be considered in the context of the *Roi de Bohême;* published separately, as they so often were, and as they still are in the 1961 Garnier edition, the idea of parody is lost on the reader, and they are then considered merely straightforward tales in the manner of *Jean-François les Bas-Bleus* or *Une Heure ou la Vision*. The narration of *Les Aveugles de Chamouny* is often interrupted by asides, questions sometimes asked, comments sometimes made, by someone called Victorine (a saucy wench no doubt), and by many false starts and digressions that the narrator does not hesitate to acknowledge. Even when the narrator lets Gervais, the blind youth, tell his tale of woe and lost love, he is often forced to silence for several pages to permit the narrator to proceed with his philosophical disquisition on, say, the etymological origin and the psychological significance of the green ribbon that covered the eyes of Eulalie after her operation to regain her sight. After Gervais has almost reached the end of his story and the narrator has promised to investigate the whereabouts of Eulalie, he summarizes calmly for us, as though he had all the time in the world at his disposal, the many side trips he, together with the narrator, had taken. Indeed, while Gervais was quietly waiting to resume his story, the reader and the protagonists have had a closing at the theater of Girolamo, a trip to Timbuctoo, a sort of excursion to Egypt, and a séance at the Institute. Eventually we are allowed to get back to our two blind people. But we are once again interrupted by a long reference to Patricia, a mare, which leaves the reader confused as to whether Breloque and others had mounted Patricia, the mare, or Patricia, a woman. But Nodier, always helpful, solves our confusion by saying: "And that's what comes from the vanity of women and mares," [28] leaving little doubt in the mind of the reader to what species Patricia belongs. In this section there is also an allusion to Don Quixote and Rosinante. Then the narrator proceeds to make a testament, *à la* Villon, and even allocates time. Finally, the mention of the word spaniel introduces the reader to the story of Brisquet's dog.

Toward the end of the book, under the heading "Invention," Nodier again demonstrates his experimental and avant-gardist vein. Here Théodore/Nodier constructs a poem composed of sounds which, he feels, "hides, under the appearance of a clever game, the most powerful creative imagination." [29] Just as words, arranged on a page, can convey visually an added dimension to meaning, so do sounds convey orally a meaning that goes beyond the initial word. Imagine, says Nodier, that you are sitting idly in a coach, perhaps you are its sole occupant; suddenly you are diverted by the sound of the coach as it stops. This is what you hear:

> Pif paf piaf patapan
> Ouhiyns ouhiyns. Ebrohé broha broha. Ouhiyns ouhiyns.
> Hoé hu. Dia hurau. Tza tza tza.
> Cla cla cla. Vli vlan. Flic flac. Flaflaflac.
> Tza tza tza. Psi psi psi. Ouistle.
> Zou lou lou. Blurlurlu. Ouistle.
> Cla cla cla. Flaflaflac.
> Ta ta ta. Ta ta ta. Pouf.
> Ouhiyns. Ebrohé broha. Ouhiyns ouhiyns.
> Ta ta-ta ta-ta ta—ta ta—hup.
> A u ho. Tza tza tza. O hem. O hup. O war!
> Trrrrrrrrrrrrrrr. Hup. O hep. O hup. O hem. Hap!
> Trrrrrrrrrrrrrrr. O hup. O hé. O halt! O! Oooooh!
> Xi xi xi xi! Pic! Pan! Baoûnd.
> Hourra!!!!!!!! [30]

As Nodier states in his analysis of the poem, it is the sound of horses that you hear as they impatiently paw the ground; then they whinney "Ouhiyns! Ouhiyns!" (their language is strangely reminiscent of Swift's horses). The coachman, Automédon, warns his impatient horses with his voice and then with the crack of the whip, but he does not touch them. The horses are impatient to enter the courtyard where they know they will get some fodder. The coach and horses cross the bridge; its wooden planks tremble with their weight. Then you are inside, the door of the château opens, you hear voices. Hurray, you are there. This is, indeed, a pleasant and amusing game, and Nodier does not hesitate to say so. But it is also an experimentation with form, an attempt to express an emotion in a novel and imaginative way. Nodier is attempting to portray an ordinary, natural tableau, the arrival of a coach after a long journey, not through the usual customary words, but through sound, that is, the sound of the words convey the idea. Aside from being a considerable feat of the imagination, the poem also reveals Nodier's constant interest in onomatopoeia or mimicry, which denotes that there is an analogy between the words man uses and the sounds he hears in nature. It is, in a sense, analogous to the concept of an original language expressed by Court de Gébelin and a number of Illuminists of the eighteenth century. Nodier was extremely interested in language and in linguistics and has written numerous articles on the origin and evolution of language. In his preface to *La Fée aux miettes* Nodier defends the simple, natural language of the people, even *argot* and *patois,* regretting that progress and modern education had contributed to their disappearance. Language, says Nodier/Théodore in defense of the poem he had just composed and which the listeners considered sheer insanity, language is something sacred, it is "imitative and descriptive poetry." [31]

At the end of *Le Roi de Bohême,* in a section entitled "Correction," Nodier once more returns to a discussion of "pantoufle." Thus the book ends, getting the seal of approval by Raminagrobis who declares that "the said work is neither impious, nor obscene, neither seditious nor satirical and as a consequence it is pleasant in a mediocre way." But, adds Raminagrobis, "the Table of Contents is very inventive and pleasant as well as very convenient to solemn religious and conservative societies which try, during winter evenings by a fire, the edifying and instructive game of *corbillon.*" [32]

## VII  Polichenelle (*1831*)

Nodier's essay on Polichinelle comes, indeed, as a surprise. Although the name of Polichinelle, Pulcinella, Punchinella, Punch, Kasper, and the like, has been the favorite of the young, he has

never been seriously discussed as a literary type until 1831 with
the appearance of Nodier's essay. He was, of course, considered as
a character in the *Commedia dell' arte* and his nature and functions were analyzed in this context. He was not, however, discussed
as a literary type the way Werther, René, Falstaff, or Hamlet were
analyzed. Obviously, Polichinelle is a great favorite with Nodier,
not merely as the amusing and quaint little character saying funny
things from his little wooden crate and whose legs one never sees,
but as an "eternal and real type," and as a "great practical moral-
ist." [33] And no one, Nodier reflects—not even Pierre Bayle who
greatly admired and loved Polichinelle—ever thought of writing
his biography. Consequently, says Nodier, he will write an essay,
for perhaps his age, that is, the nineteenth century, will be more
appreciative and understanding of Polichinelle. (It should be
added that Nodier also devoted some pages of the *Roi de Bohême*
to Polichinelle.) Polichinelle, above all, is that character with the
special laugh, who has a voice "that is not the voice of a man, . . .
but, rather, which announces something superior to man," [34]
superior because he emerged from the world of the imagination,
the dream, because he never gets old, and because he is eternally
reborn. Polichinelle does not belong to the innocents of Nodier;
neither does he belong to the "dériseurs sensés." Too cynical and
witty to belong exclusively to the former, he is also too imbued
with the sense of the fantastic and the marvelous to belong totally
to the latter. Yet, like the innocents, he, too, "occupies the highest
point in modern society." [35] Indeed, Polichinelle harbors within his
breast manifold mysteries and truths and is endowed with a keen
sense of observation and a keen sensibility. It was undoubtedly he
who suggested to Byron that a religious system could never survive two thousand years; and it was very likely Polichinelle who
whispered some of his ideas to Pascal. Polichinelle is eternal and
thus not vulnerable to the limitations that the human condition
has imposed upon man; he has successfully revolted against the
restrictions of time and space, of disintegration and death. That is
why he will never come down from his box to mingle with the
crowds; for to mingle is to become vulnerable.

But Polichinelle is also human. He, too, gets angry and impatient and has bouts with his wife and with the devil. He, too,
makes mistakes and says stupid things.

Polichinelle is like the great men of all ages: he is capricious, fantastic, touchy; Polichinelle is basically melancholy. A bitter experience, derived from the perversity of the human species, made him hostile to his fellow men; it soon turned into disdain and insulting irony which prevented him from getting involved in the trivialities of society. He consents to communicate with society but only from the top of his oblong hut and he makes fun of the vain curiosities of the crowds who pursue him, but without finding him, behind the old rug with which he covers himself.[36]

Polichinelle represents humanity as a whole; he is man in his most elemental and innermost being. He is primitive man as yet untainted by the veneer of civilization. "The story of Polichinelle," says Nodier, "is, also, the entire story of man, with all his blind beliefs, his blind passions, his blind follies, and his blind joys." [37] In Nodier's description of Polichinelle one is constantly aware of the fact that the varied characteristics given to Polichinelle could easily be given to Nodier. Both are "judicious mockers"; both can see through the foibles and vanities of men; both can make fun of themselves; and both are impatient, touchy, disdainful, and aloof. Above all, both have that simplicity and childlike innocence that is their strength and their vulnerability.

In his appreciation of and love for the character Polichinelle, Nodier demonstrates once again that he is ahead of his time and that he can be considered a precursor of those later innocents, Alfred Jarry and Guillaume Apollinaire, who also looked at the world with the eyes of a child. These two men, as did Nodier before them, tried to reassert the world of the child with its sense of the fantastic and the marvelous, with its candor and ability to believe, its spontaneity and even its ability to hurt and destroy.

## VIII  *Histoires progressives*

After writing *Le Roi de Bohême*, Nodier's satire becomes considerably more biting. In the tales *Hurlubleu, Leviathan le Long, Zerothoctro-Schah,* and *Voyage . . . dans le Paraguay-Roux,* which constitute his "*histoires progressives*" and which actually follow a continuous story line, we witness Nodier's most extensive attack on modern society and its belief in the idea of progress and perfectibility. It is with immense pleasure that Nodier ridicules pedantic fools who use words that are impressive sounding but

utterly meaningless. The discussion in *Hurlubleu* between the great
Manifafa and his servant Berniquet, "deputy of intellectual propaganda on perfectibility" and "great rascal of the sacred college of
*mataquins*" [38] is reminiscent of the arguments presented and used
by Rabelais. Trying to sound convincing to his master Manifafa,
Berniquet, in his attempt to resolve the problem of whether the
embryo of a bat is enclosed in a white or a red egg, pronounces:

> I answered smartly to Your Most Serene Highness that the two ras-
> cals had lied about it and I proved by conclusive reasoning that the
> celestial tretrapod could not have been hatched from a white egg, any
> more than it could have been hatched from a red egg, since it was by
> nature viviparous, mammalian, and anthropormorphous, neither more
> nor less than a *mataquin;* . . .[39]

Continuing in the same pedantic vein, Berniquet adds: "I knew
abstractedly in my capacity of sworn doctor of all instilled doctrines and as encyclical propagator of the perfectional monopoly
*in omni re scibili.*"

*Hurlubleu* and its sequel *Leviathan le Long* deal with Berniquet's adventures to and on the beautiful and idyllic island of
Patagonia. Embarked on a steamship named *The Progressive* with
eleven peers in search of the perfect man and the perfect society,
all types of mishaps occur. The ultimate misfortune occurs when
Berniquet is given a dose of sugar water which puts him to sleep
for ten thousand years. Upon his awakening he is sent by Leviathan le Long, King of the Patagonians, to the kingdom of
Hurlubière, whose capital is built on the ancient site of Paris, to
continue his search for the perfect man and the perfect society.
Although he has difficulty finding him, he discovers that the perfect man had almost become a reality and that this perfect man
had been fabricated by Zerothoctro-Schah almost four thousand
years ago. Unfortunately, the formula for this perfect man got lost
in a bottle of ink.

In *Zerothoctro-Schah,* the narrator and the man who had been
the porter of the Tower of Babel, discuss universal education, the
idea of progress and perfectibility, medical men, death, palingenesis, and a host of other philosophical, metaphysical, and social topics. They also discuss the French Academy. (It should,
perhaps, be mentioned that the many digs on the part of Nodier

against the French Academy did not prevent him from eventually
becoming one of its members in 1833.) Mention is also made in
this tale of our good friend Breloque, one of Nodier's alter egos in
*Le Roi de Bohême*. Berniquet also appears on the scene; he has
finally succeeded in finding his way through a bottomless tunnel.
This last part of the trilogy contains some exceedingly surreal and
fantastic scenes. Berniquet meets a little dwarf who, when inundated with fire, is resurrected.

"This deluge of fire," he tells the narrator, "with which you inundated
me, is my atmosphere and my element. Its warmth cheered me up and
I feel myself shining once more in all my ancient philosophical splendor. I owe you my palingenesis, and I will keep you informed, if I can,
of the eventual progress of a world to come." [40]

Fire has, with Nodier, as it has with Hoffmann and Nerval, resur-
rective and life-giving powers; it was as important in the work-
shop of Vulcan as it was to Prometheus. Eventually, we discover
that this dwarf is none other than Zoroaster, reformer and sage of
Persian mythology, who has been resurrected. At the end of the
tale he tells the narrator: "I am Zoroaster." This simple, final
statement is, according to Castex,[41] the key to Nodier's conception
of perfectibility. Rather than believe in the idea of the perfectibility of man or society, Nodier believes in the idea of palingenesis
or resurrection, that is, the idea of an eternal return, which he
opposes to the idea of perfectibility of the species man. This idea
will be further developed in his mystical works.

In *Voyage . . . au Paraguay-Roux* Nodier attacks such institutions as the railways, the postal service, and saving banks. Of the
latter institution, he says: "The moral force of this sublime institution has so prevailed among the population that a multitude of
individuals have decided to live on the installment plan in order
to save more." [42] And this venerable institution from which one
borrows to save is the very soul of representative governments
who know that "they have a long time to live and who feel the
need to save for the era of decadence to which they will return, by
the very nature of things, into the puerile imbecility of an earlier
age." [43] In this work Nodier is actually making fun of the little
mechanical king (the work is dated 1836 when France was gov-

erned by Louis-Philippe, the bourgeois king, a king who specu-
lated on the stock market), justice, and representative government where "the sixty-thousandth part of the nation represents
the one-hundred and fiftieth in the perspective of the one-
hundred and forty-nine others, and to their unanimous satisfac-
tion." [44]

## IX   L'Homme et la fourmi (*1833*)

It is not always easy to place the work of Nodier into categories
and cycles, for many of his tales and essays simply will not fit
neatly into little pigeonholes that the literary historian has built
for the convenience of his colleagues and students. *La plus petite
des pantoufles, Le Roi de Bohême, Polichinelle* posed such diffi-
culties. Other works such as *Paul et la ressemblance, Inès de las
Sierras,* and *L'Homme et la fourmi* pose similar problems.
*L'Homme et la fourmi,* written in 1833, because of its date of
publication and subject matter, justifies its insertion into this
group of works. It is a condemnation of the species man and a
nostalgia for a primitive world. Nodier's account of genesis, as
seen in this work, is both beautiful and terrible. The title sums up
all the lost illusions and the melancholy of the author and the
age.

The world was so beautiful before man came along! . . . When man
arrived on earth, naked, apprehensive, fearful, but already ambitious,
greedy, full of impatient agitation and power, the animals looked at
him with surprise, scattered away from him, and allowed him to pass.[45]

And wheresoever man passed he caused desolation and chaos,
and nature could be heard uttering loud cries of pain. Man was
soon able to subjugate all the animals under his yoke, for God had
given him intelligence, "an infirmity peculiar to this miserable
species." [46] But one creature man could not control: the ant
Termes and all its tribes. In the end it was the ant that brought
about the decline of man and his cities. The ant was victorious
because of its ability to be patient; therefore the ant is eternal.
With prophetic insight Nodier envisages the decline of man with
all his complexities, and the survival of the simple forms of life.
This simple tale expresses beautifully Nodier's yearning for a
primitive paradise, a yearning similar to that of Nerval, Baude-

laire, Rimbaud, Lautréamont, Jarry, and Apollinaire; a yearning that gripped the Surrealists and that grips man so forcefully to-day. All eventually came to realize that only the imagination, the world of the dream, could fulfill this terrible yearning.

CHAPTER 7

# The Mystical Works

## I  Historical Background

THE eighteenth century *Philosophes, Encyclopédists,* and *Physiocrates,* in an attempt to do away with intolerance, superstition, bigotry, and other evils, looked at the occult sciences, the supernatural, theosophy, illuminism, magic, and so on, with much derision and considered them equally absurd, meaningless, and backward as they did superstitions, intolerance, and other ills they were combating. In their attempt to place reason, logic, and the natural sciences on a pedestal and see man as a machine and thought as merely an extension of matter, they could not and would not accept notions that were not based on empirical evidence or had not passed the rigors and strains of logic. Likewise, the traditional religions of the west, Catholicism, in particular, equally decried interest in the occult sciences, magic, Oriental cults and mysteries, primarily because they felt that their own doctrines and teachings were the only valid ones and that these new ideas would conflict and compete with them. This, of course, was nothing new. Catholicism had always condemned deviations from the rigidly prescribed view. It had condemned, for example, the Quietists with equal force when it was discovered that the followers of Quietism sought and preached a very personal religion. Quietism is the expression of a religion that attempts a return to the pure and apostolic Church of God. It is a personal, individualistic religion that stresses the most inner self and a direct relationship between the individual and God. Its teachings are based on direct revelation and inspiration, which eliminates the need for an intermediary to interpret these teachings.

Nonetheless, despite the attacks and the mockery emanating from the *Philosophes* on the one hand, and the established Church, on the other, interest in the occult sciences and in Oriental mysticism and cults began to develop. Man has always wanted to know and since knowledge, that is, scientific knowledge of the physical world, as Faust was soon to realize, seemed so limited and limiting, the occult sciences, it was felt, might permit man to go beyond the world of appearances and enable him to overcome the strictures of knowledge and the limitations of the mind. The world of the supernatural and the occult sciences could perhaps afford man to break the chains tying him to time and space. By studying the occult sciences man could, perhaps, overcome the terrible enigma: the nature of death and life after death.

During the last thirty years of the eighteenth century, interest in the Orient and in Oriental religions, cults, philosophies, literature, language began to manifest itself in Germany, France, and England. Works such as the *Upanishads,* the *Bhagavad-Gita,* the *Ramayana, Sakuntala,* and many others, were discovered and translated by European scholars; sometimes, unfortunately, they were interpreted by pseudoscholars. Thus the discovery of these works emanating from the Orient brought Western scholars and thinkers for the first time face to face with ideas that were not steeped in Aristotelian logic, Cartesian rationalism, and Euclidian concepts of space. With the emergence of Hindu, Persian, and Chinese thought in Western Europe, the ideas of the Middle East, such as Kabbala, Gnosticism, and Neo-Platonism were also revitalized. It was this philosophical, theological, and literary meeting of Eastern and Western thought that gave rise to Illuminism.

## II *Illuminism*

Illuminism did not come into being in the eighteenth century. A group in Spain calling itself the *Alumbrados* already existed at the end of the fifteenth century. However, the Spanish Inquisition saw to it that its members were stamped out by burning them at the stake or by other such ingenious methods of eradication. Many members managed to escape to France where a more friendly climate existed. Quietism, which was founded by the Spanish monk Molinos, was certainly linked to Spanish Illuminism. Besides having its origins in the *Alumbrados,* Quietism, and Oriental mystical cults and religion, Illuminism was also influenced by Neo-Platonism. Thus Platonism and the Platonic Idea of archetypes once more began to play an important role. Illuminism, as the word implies, attempts to illuminate, to bring the light. Coming toward the end of the Age of Enlightenment and Reason, an

age which attempted to enlighten in quite a different manner, Illuminism is also an attempt to refute the empirical world and rationalism.

Illuminism, like Romanticism, concerned itself with the discovery of man's inner self, the unconscious, and with the impact of
the dream on the psychic life of man. It was felt that all man's
riches, all his possessions, in fact, his whole universe, lay within
the deep recesses of his mind. The Illuminists, like the Romanticists, and like the Platonists before them, saw the poet once again
as a nocturnal seer and prophet, divinely inspired. The poet, like
the magician and diviner of ancient times, was able to see into the
invisible and impalpable world, the world behind the world of
appearances, that is, the unconscious. Thus, the poet is like the
seer of old who sees poetry in magic as well as magic in poetry.
German Romanticists such as Novalis, Achim von Arnim, E. T. A.
Hoffmann, and French Romanticists such as Nodier, Nerval,
Baudelaire, and Rimbaud all believed that the artist, or the poet,
was a seer and that poetry had as its mission the re-creation of this
primitive language, which is part of man's unconscious, hidden in
the deep recesses of the mind. The universality of this primitive
language and this primitive alphabet is assured, they thought, because everything in both the physical and the mental world is the
expression of the unconsciousness of a supreme being, a supreme
mind or soul, which is the one and only consciousness that exists.

Some of the cults and doctrines that made a considerable impact on the thinking of the eighteenth and nineteenth centuries
were Kabbala, Gnosticism, Manicheism, and Pythagoreanism.
Kabbala consists of a series of books composed of mystical teachings, commentaries, and rituals which play an important role in
the rituals and doctrines of the Freemasons and the Rosicrucians.
Gnosticism is primarily concerned with the acquisition of knowledge of an esoteric sort and makes an effort to transcend rational,
logical thought process by means of intuition. Manicheism, like
Gnosticism, is concerned with illuminating man about the secrets
of nature and fighting the dark powers. Pythagoreanism conceived of man as having a dual nature—body and soul—and
believed in the immortality and transmigration of the soul; the Py-
thagoreans also believed that all phenomena were sensuous expressions of mathematical ratios—that is, they believed there existed a correspondence between numbers and things. This concept

of correspondences influenced enormously Illuminists and Romanticists alike. Political and social Illuminism found expression in such secret societies as Freemasonry, Rosicrucianism, both very much influenced by Kabbala and Pythagoreanism. Both these societies hoped to combine Christian mysticism and ethics with the occult and theosophy of the Orient. Cults such as mesmerism and galvanism concerned themselves with animal magnetism; syncretism was a belief in a universal, primitive religion; metempsychosis or avatarism conceived of the soul as being able to successively reside in more than one body, and later was incorporated in the idea of palingenesis, which means successive resurrection; metapsychosis, or mental telepathy, believes that a mind has a force over another. Other cults such as the worship of Osiris, associated with the idea of reincarnation and which overlaps with Orphism and the cult of the goddess Isis, are also linked to the idea of death and rebirth. Already with the cult of Isis we have come in contact with the idea of syncretism, Isis being considered a universal figure, the mother goddess in whom are personified all the other goddesses of the Mediterranean world. The worship of Osiris and Isis is at the basis of Freemasonry and Rosicrucianism. All these cults, theosophies, and philosophies, emanating from Greece, Egypt, Persia, and Spain found their way eventually into the thinking and writings of the Illuminists of the eighteenth century and many Romanticists of the nineteenth century.

One of the most important Illuminists to influence the writers of the nineteenth century and whose influence can be compared to that of Kierkegaard's influence on the French and German writers of the twentieth century, was Emmanuel Swedenborg (1688–1772). His cosmology rests primarily on the notion of correspondences, a notion already apparent in Pythagoreanism. As Swedenborg sees it, there exists a correspondence between the material, physical universe and the spiritual universe, the universe of pure thought. That is, every phenomenon in the world of nature has its counterpart in the spiritual world. It is by means of this correspondence that man can communicate with heaven. This idea of correspondences or analogies contains the idea of "sympathetic" attractions, introduced through the discovery of magnetism; it was soon attributed to other facets of life: nature and its corresponding symbols and numbers, music, architecture, colors, and sounds. Even man became an analogy since he was the microcosm

in which the macrocosm reflected itself. The idea of correspondences or analogies in all its forms and variations influenced such
writers as Nodier, Nerval, Baudelaire, Balzac, Rimbaud, and
many others. Swedenborg also introduced the idea of a universal
language, an idea he expounded in *The Language of the Angels,*
which forms part of *Heaven and Hell.* To discover this universal
language is to discover the mysteries of nature. This archetypal,
universal language is the one to which all earthly languages corre-
spond. It cannot be learned but must be intuited; it is instantane-
ous, telepathic.

An important scholar and contributor to the dissemination of
Oriental languages and philosophies was Court de Gébelin (1725–
84) whose eight-volume work, entitled *The Primitive World*
(1772), contributed enormously to an understanding of the Orient. He was one of the first to develop the idea of the purity of
Oriental religions. Gébelin felt that the religions of the Orient
were purer because they were more "primitive," that is, closer to
the source. He compares this primitive religion to water that is
purest when closest to its source. With Swedenborg, Gébelin believed in the idea that there is a primitive, original language of
nature at the basis of all languages. The various alphabets, he felt,
derived from a single alphabet, the alphabet of nature. The idea
of a single language and a single alphabet, a single religion, and a
single poetic language that one can find in nature has influenced
German as well as French Romanticists.

Nodier's interest in Illuminism and contact with some aspects of
Illuminism goes back to his early childhood. It was primarily due
to his father's friendship with Jacques Cazotte, who was a frequent visitor to the Nodier household, which brought Nodier in
contact with the ideas of such Illuminists as Martinez de Pas-
qually and Saint-Martin, men who, in turn, had influenced
Jacques Cazotte. Other Illuminists with whom Nodier came in
contact were Swedenborg, Johannes Hamann, and Jean Lavater.
Two men who influenced Nodier immensely with respect to the
idea of palingenesis were Pierre-Simon Ballanche and Charles Bonnet. Bonnet in his *Palingénésie philosophique,* indicates a belief in
the existence of a future state, a state after death, and that all
living beings, animals included, can, through metempsychosis, attain a higher level. It is by this means that man can attain perfectibility. Ballanche, on the other hand, was more concerned with

the idea of palingenesis as it applied to societies. In his *Essais de palingénésie sociale* (1830), Ballanche says that societies would improve by a process of palingenesis and advocates the fusion of all Christendom. Another influence on Nodier was Bonneville with *Les Jésuites chassés de la maçonnerie* (1788) and *L'Esprit des religions* (1791).

Nodier's interest in Illuminism is already evident in his early works. In *Une Heure ou la Vision,* the idea of palingenesis is already apparent, although in a more superficial manner. The idea of the poet or madman as endowed with the special gift of voyancy is already visible in *Jean-François les Bas-Bleus, L'Histoire d'Hélène Gillet, La Fée aux miettes,* and *Baptiste Montauban ou l'Idiot.* These ideas will become more and more dominant when his attitude toward life and the world becomes more desperate and the need for consolation becomes more urgent and more persistent to his well-being, mentally as well as physically.

## III   De la Palingénésie humaine et la résurrection (*1832*)[1]

Although written in 1832, this work can serve as a key to his later works, those dealing with death and resurrection and which Castex calls the mystical cycle of Nodier. To the idea of progress and perfectibility of man and society, Nodier opposes the idea of human palingenesis, an idea already evident in Hinduism with its concept of reincarnation and transmigration and in Pythagoreanism with its concept of metempsychosis. Palingenesis differs from metempsychosis in that the latter assumes that the same soul successively resides in more than one body, human or animal; palingenesis, on the other hand, expresses the idea of resurrection, not of the same soul assuming another body, but of the resurrection of another species. Nodier's concept of human palingenesis differs from that of Bonnet or Ballanche. According to Bonnet, thanks to the progress of metempsychosis, all living things, even those low on the evolutionary scale, can attain a higher state or level; Ballanche differs to a considerable extent in his concept of palingenesis, for he is primarily interested in taking the idea of rebirth or resurrection and applying it to society.

Nodier, at the very outset of this essay, makes it clear that he is not concerned with social palingenesis or resurrection, for these two concepts, "genesis" and "society," are contradictory. "Genesis" is, after all, the process of creation and involves a supreme being or power, whereas "society" is the work of instinct and forms an integral part of the human species. Man made his society according to his needs and to the best of his ability, no more and no less. The attainment of perfection in man and society does not constitute an integral part of the nature of the human species. Perfectibility is, after all, Godlike, and man is, at best, imperfect. In this essay Nodier once again expresses the idea of the end or decline of the human species: "If man's destiny is not completed, it is because man is not the end of creation. He is only a fleeting episode whose destiny lies hidden in the outcome of universal action." [2]

Man, says Nodier, is the most miserable of all creatures, first because he, alone, knows that he will die, secondly, because he does not have the necessary organs with which to comprehend the notion of death. Man, because he is a rational creature, is limited by the very process that makes him superior to the animals: reason. It is this thought process that makes him aware of three contingencies: creation, space, and time. Man's problems stem from the fact that he is not a comprehensive being but merely man, a thinking being, with all its limitations. As a rational being, man can conceive of resurrection but merely as something anticipatory, which he can comprehend with his reason but not with his senses. To the new species, the comprehensive being, the notion of resurrection will be perfectly comprehensible and will form part of his experience. The Church, says Nodier, early recognized man's need for a state beyond the state on earth, and conceived the idea of purgatory and judgment as a state between life and resurrection. The Church also recognized in the angel man's need for a comprehensive being. Thus this new species, this comprehensive being, will be akin to an angel. Nodier is emphatic about distinguishing the species man from the comprehensive being; this comprehensive being is by no means man, perfected, but a completely different species.

This comprehensive being, according to Nodier, will be created on the sixth day. It is interesting to find Nodier interpreting the Bible in his own way. The Bible, says Nodier, is not based on dogmatic facts, but merely on apparent facts, relative to man's notions and interpretations at a particular time and place. For example, Genesis mentions that God created the world in seven days. This should not be taken to mean seven days composed of twenty-four hours as we know and conceive of time. Time, in the Bible, says Nodier, has a totally different nature.

Man has difficulty comprehending the existence of God because man, this rational being, has organs that are not complete and therefore man is incapable of understanding and accepting such concepts. Nodier sees the evolution from the species man to the comprehensive being as part of a great chain of being: the mineral evolved into the plant; the plant into the animal with its developed senses; the animal into man with the developed brain; man will develop into the comprehensive being with its three intelligential senses: memory, imagination, and judgment; finally, the comprehensive being will evolve into a state of resurrection which will be a final and permanent state. Thus, it is obvious that, according to Nodier, creation is not completed and to speak of man evolving into a perfect being is erroneous; rather, the species man is reaching its end and a new species will take his place.

Nodier then reflects on the characteristics of the comprehensive being. He will be superior to man, just as man is superior to the beast. He will, on the other hand, resemble man in some ways, just as man resembles the beast in many ways. The comprehensive being will differ from man through the development of an organ or organs unknown to man. On the other hand, this new being will most likely lose certain organs that man possesses, just as man lost certain organs that animals still possess. Thus, each species gains and loses in the process of change. Furthermore, such notions as time and space will have a totally different significance to the comprehensive being and concepts such as aging, death, and immortality will be meaningless terms.

How and when will this change take place? How long does it last? Since time will have a different meaning, the process will be timeless and could occur almost instantaneously. "It is only death," [3] says Nodier. Death, which brings about the change from the state of life to the state of a pure being, or a comprehensive being, is not something one should fear. Unfortunately, the traditional notion of the *néant*, of nothingness, causes man to fear and tremble, for man considers the *néant* as the opposite of resurrection. According to Nodier, people laugh at the notion of resurrection, and, indeed, the traditional notion man has of resurrection is pathetic because it is limited by man's inability to comprehend and conceive of the state of resurrection. On the contrary, the idea of resurrection should make man happy for it is a state of eternity, a state where space, time, duration, the *néant*, the past, future, no longer exist. Only the present exists, the "sense of a being prolonged forever." [4] Furthermore, says Nodier, it is only then that concepts such as creation and God will become clear. In the final analysis, adds Nodier, if you prefer my tales to my philosophy, I will comply and tell you some tales. And Nodier proceeds to tell us a few tales that deal with palingenesis. Thus, Illuminism and theosophy become literary.

## IV   Paul ou la ressemblance (*1836*)

It has not always been easy to draw a clear line of demarcation between the works of Nodier, in particular with respect to his works after 1830. Whereas *Lydie ou la résurrection* and *Franciscus Columna* clearly belong to Nodier's mystical works of the later years, tales such as *Paul ou la ressemblance* and *Légende de Soeur Béatrix* are more difficult to assess. On the surface *Paul ou la ressemblance* seems very much like a traditional tale not even imbued with the fantastic, an "histoire véritable et fantastique," as the subtitle claims it is.

The story is as follows. An old man on horseback follows a coach occupied by the Marquis de Louvois and his young servant, Paul. When the nobleman and Paul arrive at the inn to rest and dine, they find the old man also present. While the Marquis is at table, he is approached by the old man who tells him his story. He is in search of his son Paul who has died recently. However, his wife had a vision of the Virgin announcing to her that their son is still alive; this convinces the old man, who sets out to search for his son. In his search, he sees Paul who is the exact double of his son, and the old man now believes firmly that the Virgin has kept her promise and has returned to them their dead son. Unfortunately, the Marquis has to disillusion the old man about the origins of his servant Paul who has a father and a background of his own. The old man finally understands that Paul is not his son; nevertheless, he offers to adopt Paul, promising him money, a nice home, and the love of two parents. But Paul declines the offer, wanting to remain loyal to his own father, who, though poor, is still his real father, and to his memories. He says that he cannot adopt the life of another individual because he has lived his life and loved people and things known only to him; to occupy the life of another is impossible.

On this level, the story is neither fantastic nor mystical, for resemblances of this type are not unusual. However, it is the context in which this tale is placed and the final statements Nodier makes about death and resurrection that permit one to place this tale with the mystical works of Nodier. Furthermore, two events that occur in the tale justify placing it with *Lydie* and *Franciscus Columna:* the vision of the Virgin and the prophecy made to Paul that he would obtain a fortune in the Pyrenees. The Marquis de Louvois is greatly struck by these two coincidences, and although he is a man of the world and does not believe in such occurrences, he, nevertheless, does not deny the possibility of such phenomena. Nodier, himself, neither accepts nor denies the validity of these two coincidences and merely states that they give him much cause to reflect. But Nodier also uses the opportunity to attack the philosophical positivists and the rationalists of his age:

Positivist philosophers who deny the intervention of God in earthly matters will give credit to the power of chance for these extraordinary occurrences, since chance is the name given to God by those who have taken the desperate stand not to believe in him. Christians will see in such occurrences a more comforting and higher meaning.[5]

Nodier ends this tale with a lengthy discussion of death and the consolation afforded one when one believes in life after death and the resurrection of the body. He then recounts another tale about a man called Lazarus Néobius, an Irishman, who died some time ago. After lying for ten days in his coffin, he arose from the dead and lived for another ten years. He also managed to record these experiences in a book which Nodier has in his possession. Resurrection, Nodier is thereby saying, is not so uncommon and happens quite frequently throughout history.

## V  Légende de Soeur Béatrix (1837)

This little tale is more in keeping with what is considered a miracle tale of the Middle Ages and thus can more appropriately be placed among Nodier's mystical works. The tale centers around a miracle performed by the Virgin for sister Béatrix. But first

Nodier devotes a number of pages discussing the afflictions and evils that beset this age, attributing man's ills to the disappearance of faith, enthusiasm, love, charity, and, above all, to the disappearance of man's sense of poetry and the imagination.

The poetry of an age is, indeed, composed of two essential elements, the genuine faith of the man of imagination who believes in what he tells and the genuine faith of men of feeling who believe what they hear. Outside of this state of mutual confidence and understanding, in which well assorted intelligences come to merge, poetry is but an empty word, the fruitless and futile art of measuring some sonorous syllables in orderly rhythms. There lies the reason why we no longer have poetry in the true and original meaning of the word, and why we will not have it for a long time to come, if ever.[6]

This attack on disbelief and lack of poetry is, of course, part of Nodier's incessant disgust with an age that believes in scientism and has faith in the idea of progress and perfectibility. But placed at the head of the story itself, it is a rather ingenious device on the part of Nodier to force the reader to try to believe what he tells us, especially if the reader has the typical attitudes of the age with respect to science and technology and also possibly harbors a skepticism that will make him doubt the tale.

In the Jura mountains stands the convent of Notre-Dame-des-Épines-Fleuries. Noted in the chronicles of the convent is the occurrence of a miracle two hundred years ago when the convent's most saintly nun was visited by the Virgin. The presence of the Virgin was made apparent when a crude wooden statue of the Virgin was suddenly enveloped in a halo of light. To honor the Virgin, this statue was then placed in an elegant niche in the chapel of the convent. However, the following day, the niche was empty; the statue had disappeared. It was presumed that the Virgin preferred her more modest domicile. Two centuries later a young nun, sister Béatrix, is in charge of taking care of the tabernacle in honor of the Virgin. But sister Béatrix, as fate would have it, meets a young man in distress; he had been attacked by robbers just outside the convent and was in need of first aid. Sister Béatrix, a capable nurse, manages to revive the young man. He turns out to be her childhood sweetheart, Raymond. He accuses her of being unfaithful and of having betrayed her "destiny as mistress, spouse, and mother."[7] Raymond argues well and con-

vinces sister Béatrix that she should follow him and remain with
him forever. A year of bliss goes by in which sister Béatrix experiences love and a worldly life. But soon Béatrix realizes that Raymond no longer loves her. Indeed, he soon leaves her. Fifteen
years of solitude, misery, and vice go by. Finally Béatrix decides
that she prefers to beg among people she does not know. After
days of wandering, she suddenly finds herself back at the convent.
She is given food and a place to sleep by one of the nuns. At the
convent, Béatrix suddenly discovers that the Virgin, during her
absence, had taken her form and replaced her at the tabernacle.
She then meets the Virgin face to face, who tells her to return to
her post and to don her habit which she will find in her former
cell. By donning her former habit Béatrix also clothes herself with
her earlier innocence. "It is an uncommon grace that I owe you
for your love, and that I obtain for your forgiveness. Adieu, sister
custodian of Maria! Love Mary as she loved you." [8] Thus, the
sinner Béatrix becomes once again the nun Béatrix. There is, however, some consternation among the nuns in the convent: the old
sick woman who had been given shelter and food has suddenly
disappeared. But sister Béatrix reassures the nuns and tells them
that she knows where the old woman is and that she is well and
happy. The nuns are reassured but they notice that it is the first
time that sister Béatrix has spoken in rather harsh terms.

This tale is reminiscent of the subplot of Lewis' *The Monk*, the
sad and gruesome tale told by the young lover, Raymond de las
Cisternas, who also loved a nun and attempted to elope with her.
Forming part of the subplot is also the story of the Bleeding Nun,
which is the story of Beatrice de las Cisternas, who had eloped
with a certain Baron Lindenberg and had lived with him as his
mistress for several years and then was betrayed by him. (The
episode of the Bleeding Nun was also included by Nodier in *Infernaliana*.) Although the plot remains, by 1837 the frenetic or
gothic aspects have disappeared and we have a simple and sentimental tale of the persecuted maiden imbued with mysticism.

## VI   Lydie ou la résurrection (1839)

It is primarily in *Lydie ou la résurrection* that the idea of palingenesis is most clearly and dramatically expressed. Lydie, a young
wife, has lost her husband in a fire as he attempted to save a
mother and her four children. The villagers, although they are

sorry for her, consider her mad because she insists that she communicates each night with her husband who conducts her into the world beyond. "What is it to be mad?" asks Lydie, fully aware of her predicament and the *double vie* that she is leading. It is, Lydie answers, "a happy state, in fact, the happiest, second only to death." [9] In her misfortune at having lost her husband, she spends sleepless nights. One night she sees a light that becomes brighter and brighter; finally it is so bright that she has difficulty comprehending how the human eye can withstand such brightness. She then hears the sound of wings fluttering nearby. She soon perceives the wings and they have golden plumes and the sound of their vibration has a heavenly ring. She instinctively knows that it is her husband who has taken the form of an angel. His wings surround her, his arms envelop her, his lips seek her lips and press her forehead, her eyes—it is the same voluptuousness that we experienced in *Une Heure ou la vision*. Together they rise up into "an ocean that is without bottom and without shores, in this infinite ether that is eternally without night." [10] They are together in the world of the resuscitated, "that place where happy souls come to take other forms or undergo other tests . . . to become worthy in anticipation of the day when they can appear before God." [11] We know, however, that because George has always led an exemplary and honest life, doing good to others at the risk of his own life and happiness, that he will soon be able to see God. That is why he urges Lydie not to despair and not to contemplate suicide, which is a crime against nature and God; to make matters easier for Lydie, he suggests that when they have to part in the morning, she should consider this as though he were simply going off to fish as he had done when he was still alive. He then proceeds to explain to Lydie his state of being which is the intermediary state a person has to undergo until he has proven himself worthy of God. It should be recalled that in his essay on palingenesis, Nodier had called that state the state of the comprehensive being. Thereafter, George continues, a being will enter the resurrectional state, the state of eternity. But these moments of bliss have to end, and Lydie has to return to the world of everyday experience, the world of reality.

When Lydie awakens, she discovers that it is the doctor who is holding her hand. Incapable of comprehending the dream that Lydie has had, the doctor wants to place her in an asylum for the alienated in order to cure her. Fortunately, an old woman who loves and understands Lydie and who takes care of her, prevents this from taking place; she alone believes in the reality of what Lydie experienced during the night. To cure her, to take away from her, the world she has created for herself, would be detrimental to Lydie, for this world is as essential to her as is the air she breathes. In her misfortune this is the only consolation she has. Indeed, the world Lydie has created for herself is a superior world, a world in which death cannot affect the individual, since the transition between the world in which she lives and the world after death does not exist. Thus, death, according to Nodier, is no longer to be feared; and like the world of the imagination, the dream, it is a consolation and a refuge. Thus nothing dies; things only change their form. The threat of the *néant,* of total nothingness, no longer menaces one. In the end, when it is Lydie's turn to die, she does so happily and peacefully, for she will be with George—she, too, will enter into another eternal state.

## VII   Franciscus Columna (*1844*)

*Franciscus Columna* was published shortly after the death of Nodier. It is a story of love and fidelity and is reminiscent of the love that existed between Abelard and Heloïse, but without the sensuality of the medieval lovers. Franciscus is an artist who is soon to become a monk. He loves the beautiful, rich, and highly educated Polia. He lives in a world of the dream, a world where "love feared not the slightest vicissitudes of either fortunes or age." [12] On the day of her departure from Venice, she, too, tells Franciscus that she loves him. Nothing really prevents them from marriage except the fact that they (and Nodier with them) want to keep this love innocent and pure; both know that their separation on this earth is only temporary, for "this earth is only a fleeting place of sojourn where souls must prove themselves" [13] before they can enter eternity. This idea is reminiscent of *Trilby* where the lovers, separated for a while, are to meet again in eternity where love never dies. At the end of the tale, during a moment of pure ecstasy, and when his thoughts are directed toward his beloved Polia, Franciscus passes from the world of the dream he had created for himself into the world of eternal bliss; quite likely, he will soon be joined by Polia.

With *Lydie ou la résurrection* and *Franciscus Columna,* Nodier has come full circle. An idea that began with *Une Heure ou la vision* found its culmination in these two tales, namely, that man, after having discarded that perishable envelope he calls the body, will live in some realm of the universe in eternal bliss. Above all, he will find once again the one he had loved on earth. Love plays an important role in the works of Nodier. It is made in heaven and ends in heaven, but it is not of and for this world. It is ennobling, but it is never fulfilled. It is not the kind of love expressed by Shakespeare or the Surrealists, where, though love is also something ennobling and even made in heaven, it is also a "fine lunacy," something lawless, a rebellion against authority and parents. With Nodier love may verge on the lawless or capricious, even on the sensual and material, but, in the final analysis, it remains pure and unfulfilled. Sometimes, indeed, love has a certain erotic quality, found primarily in those works where the influence of Rabelais, Diderot, Laurence Sterne, and others, dominates. Even in the works that belong to the cycle of the *voyants*, the innocents, or the mystics, love may sometimes be imbued with sensuality; the love portrayed in *Une Heure ou la vision, Trilby, La Fée aux miettes,* and *Lydie* contains such elements. Woman may, indeed, be sensual at times; she may even be the one to communicate this sensuality to man. Nonetheless, an aura of innocence is always present. Even Folly Girlfree, the little temptress, is endowed with a purity and innocence. Nodier's woman is also the mistress-spouse-mother, the archetype of the eternal woman, the Beatrice or Goddess Isis, who guides the man she loves and helps him overcome his many trials. But she, too, retains her purity. It is, after all, not the Fée aux Miettes whom Michel touches, but Belkiss, her alter ego. Love sometimes also takes on a protective quality, the kind of love a father has for his daughter. The love Jean Sbogar/Lothario has for Antonia is an example of just such a love. His love is without passion, that is, it is without carnal passion; rather, it is something more powerful and bigger that dominates his love: a feeling of protection and the desire not to besmirch the purity and innocence of a love that has been made in heaven.

# CHAPTER 8

# *Nodier, Literary Critic*

## I *Nodier and La Quotidienne*

IT has by now become evident that Nodier's intellectual life, like his emotional life, was not without ambiguities, inconsistencies, and conflicts, arising from his own mental and physical makeup, as well as from the conflicts that existed within the age itself. Romanticist by instinct and temperament, Classicist by education and taste, as well as heir to the eighteenth century, Nodier, nonetheless, remained consistent in his valuation of literary works. In his judgment of writers and their works Nodier was, from the outset, a Romanticist. This constancy toward certain literary works becomes apparent when one reads the essays he wrote for newspapers such as *Le Journal des Débats, La Quotidienne, Le Drapeau Blanc, La Revue de Paris,* and *La Revue des Deux Mondes* and the numerous prefaces and comments inserted here and there within the pages of his *contes* and *nouvelles.* His admiration for certain writers often considered precursors of Romanticism is already evident in 1800 when he says: "Have you read Montaigne, Charron, Rabelais and Tristram Shandy? If not, read them. If you have read them, re-read them!" [1] Two years later Nodier's literary tastes are again made clear when, in *Les Proscrits,* he describes the books that are in the library of his hero. E. M. Schenck, mixing her own prose with that of Nodier, says:

The first book, the Bible—twenty-five years before the *Préface de Cromwell!*—held the first spot; next to it could be found Klopstock's *Messiah . . .* ; farther down one could distinguish Montaigne, the philosopher of the human heart, placed between Shakespeare, who is its painter, and Richardson, who is its historian; Rousseau, Sterne, and a few others followed.[2]

In a letter written to his friend Weiss in 1803, it is again the Bible, Ossian, and Werther who take first place. "Instead of Tournefort and Linnaeus, we will take with us into exile, the Bible, Ossian, Werther, Ballanche and Auguste Glaize. Men can think whatever they want; we will have the right to build in the desert a library after our heart's desire." [3]

Nonetheless, this inclination and emotional bent Nodier had for Romanticism did not prevent him from writing for conservative, monarchist newspapers such as *Le Drapeau Blanc* and *La Quotidienne*, newspapers devoted to the defense of the Bourbons, Catholicism, and Classicism, primarily motivated by politics in their literary judgments and opinions. But it was chiefly for *La Quotidienne* that Nodier devoted much time and effort. It is interesting to note that the inconsistencies and conflicts that existed within Nodier, in some measure, also existed within the pages of *La Quotidienne* and that the battles that raged in France between Classicism and Romanticism, between the proponents of the *ancien régime* and the revolution and/or Bonapartism, also raged, although in a more muted form, within the microcosm of *La Quotidienne*. What *La Quotidienne* hated above all were the ideas of Madame de Staël, especially her ideas on the perfectibility of man and society, for it implied to the editors of *La Quotidienne* that the period of the revolution was superior to the prerevolutionary period; they also hated her enthusiasm for German Romanticism. *La Quotidienne* was equally vehement in its appraisal of Benjamin Constant's *Adolphe*, which it considered an example of decadence and what can happen to an individual when he comes under the influence of that malady called the *mal de René*. However, when *Jean Sbogar* was published in 1818, *La Quotidienne* reviewed the work with considerable enthusiasm, despite the fact that it was immeasurably more imbued with the spirit of Romanticism than was *Adolphe*. Undoubtedly, here, too, *La Quotidienne* saw in *Jean Sbogar* a condemnation of a malady and assumed that Nodier was attempting to teach a moral. *La Quotidienne* went so far as to consider the ideas emanating from Albion's shores even more dangerous than those coming from beyond the Rhine, for England, it was felt, was largely responsible for the ideas that had infested eighteenth-century France politically, socially, and morally. *La Quotidienne* was equally scandalized by the theater of Shakespeare and considered it too crude for French sensibilities.

When one takes cognizance of the strong conservative opinions expressed by the editors of *La Quotidienne,* one is, indeed, surprised to discover that Nodier collaborated closely with this newspaper. We know that Nodier believed with *La Quotidienne* in Catholicism and monarchy and felt that France needed a new literature based on good, sound religious and moral principles; yet, fundamental differences existed between Nodier and his colleagues. A divergence of opinion certainly existed with respect to certain eighteenth-century writers in France and abroad. Whereas the members of *La Quotidienne* condemned the age of the *Philosophes* and blamed many of its writers for the Revolution of 1789 as well as for the decline of moral and religious principles, Nodier makes a distinction between the archrationalists and *Philosophes,* the believers in progress and perfectibility, and the pre-Romanticists such as Rousseau and Bernardin de Saint-Pierre. He also reserves a place of esteem for men like Diderot, Laclos, and Crébillon fils, whom *La Quotidienne* regarded as libertines and responsible for the deterioration of France's moral standards.

But what may at first appear as an inconsistency in Nodier may resolve itself after closer investigation. In the first place, says Helen Maxwell King, *La Quotidienne* underwent a change of heart between the years 1818 and 1824 (only to become even more conservative after 1824). Some of its editors and contributors soon came to realize that a total return to prerevolutionary days was not possible and felt bound to adapt themselves to some degree to the mood that was pervading the country, especially if they wanted to have a voice at all, and if they wanted to retain some contact with the young intellectuals and artists who had come of age during the Restoration. Furthermore, the inclusion of two men on the staff of *La Quotidienne* brought about a considerable amount of "liberalization," for these two men, Martainville and Malte-Brun,[4] gave a new perspective to the pages devoted to theater criticism. Malte-Brun, a native of Denmark, was especially valuable to the newspaper. According to King, it was he, rather than Hugo, who was the real precursor of the dramatic principles that were later expressed in the *Préface de Cromwell.* Thanks to these two men, says King, Shakespeare ceased to be regarded as a menace to French culture and began to be worthy of consideration. A third drama critic, Mély-Janin, who considered Schiller as the great genius of Romanticism, at least for a while, also contributed to this change of heart. It is interesting to see that the greatest period of "liberalization" that occurred in the pages of *La Quotidienne* coincided with the period when Nodier collaborated with that newspaper, that is, between 1821 and 1824.[5] To show their goodwill, the editors even praised Nodier's *Smarra*.[6] It is also around 1821 that Romanticism began to be regarded as a potential national French movement, associated with the making of a national French literature and synonymous with Chateaubriand, monarchy, Christianity, chivalry, and other national traditions. This was exactly what Nodier was trying to achieve for France. And so long as some of the ideas of Romanticism conformed with the ideas of *La Quotidienne*, its editors were willing to discuss, if not necessarily accept, them.

## II   *Nodier and Walter Scott*

Two writers early associated with the new movement were Walter Scott and Victor Hugo; both were palatable to the editors of *La Quotidienne*.[7] The first two articles Nodier wrote on Scott were written in connection with the publication of Scott's *Oeuvres complètes* in France. These two articles appeared in *La Quotidienne* on December 17 and 31, 1821. In these articles Nodier points out two important traits inherent in the works of Scott: first, that the works of Scott contain classical qualities; secondly, that the Romanticism of Scott is neither objectionable nor extravagant. "*Ivanhoe*," says Nodier, "is one of those books that is classical at the very outset and destined to survive in the same way that a literature survives." [8] To make *Ivanhoe* acceptable to the conservative readers of *La Quotidienne*, Nodier compared the work to Homer's *Odyssey* and Ariosto's *Orlando furioso*. Furthermore, says Nodier, there is such a thing as good and bad Romanticism and *Ivanhoe* belongs to the former. It is obvious, continues Nodier, that to develop a new literature, new forms and expressions are necessary. Each age soon discovers that it needs new forms and modes of expression with which it can express the old truths and make them more understandable to the age. This idea is repeated in another essay on Scott dated August 29, 1823 wherein Nodier condemns the critics of Scott for failing to see the value of Scott's bold descriptions and who "confused the unknown with the impossible." [9] In this article Nodier also repeats his earlier argument that Scott gave to England a sense of its own traditions, the sense of the Middle Ages, and a love of country. Is that not religion, monarchy, and morality, all bound in one? France, Nodier feels, could very well use something of this sort.

In the essays on Scott written in December 1821, Nodier also says some interesting things with respect to the novel which, he feels, is the "varied expression of a mobile society" and thus cannot be restricted by rules; rather, the novel should "modify itself in accordance with the character of the different ages, the direction and movement of its intellectual thought, the nature and intensity of the passions and follies of the age." [10] In his analysis of the novel, Nodier makes a very bold and pertinent point when he says that the revolution gave birth to a literature that was not completely reprehensible. In the hands of a Chateaubriand and a Walter Scott, the novel, almost to the point of disappearing, has been given a new impetus with newer and better characteristics making themselves more conspicuous. Thus, thanks to Romanticism, "the novel acquired a certain noble and religious authority. . . . Christianity and morality, chased away from the temples, found a refuge in literature." [11] An interesting point that Nodier makes in these articles on Scott is that there is a relationship between the terrible convulsions and upheavals that shook Europe during and after the Revolution of 1789 and the type of literature Nodier calls "frénétique" that was so popular during his day. Thus, without necessarily condoning the "genre frénétique," Nodier indicates that he at least understands the deep-seated expression of fear and anguish that permeated the literature of the time: the English gothic novel, Sade, Byron, and others. "Critics," says Nodier, "have not been sufficiently aware of the fact that this taste for romantic productions is sometimes something other than merely a mania—it is often a need, a passion. Extraordinary events must have created these extraordinary impulses in our emotions and our passions." [12]

### III   *Nodier and Victor Hugo*

The relationship between Hugo and *La Quotidienne* is, in a sense, also the relationship between Nodier and Hugo, for Nodier wrote almost all of his articles on Hugo while collaborating with *La Quotidienne*. The relationship between the two men was one that began with love and respect at first sight and ended with bitterness and sorrow, primarily on the part of Nodier. The two writers met in 1821 at a meeting of the Société Royale des Bonnes

Lettres. On this particular night, the two Hugo brothers, Abel and Victor, both ardent Royalists, read their latest literary achievements, which were greatly applauded by those present. The type of relationship that was to last for several years was immediately established, Nodier acting as mentor and protector to the much younger and more ambitious Hugo. Eager to become the new lion of the emerging movement, Hugo knew how to take advantage of the position, contacts, and experience of Nodier.

As early as 1819 *La Quotidienne* had already referred to the rising talent of Hugo, praising the good verses and noble sentiments Hugo expressed in his early odes. Brief allusions to the publication of other odes were made again in 1820, 1821, and 1822. On April 27, 1822, *La Quotidienne* announced the publication of a collection of Hugo's odes, entitled *Les Odes et Poésie diverses.* After this initial announcement there was a silence of about four months. This silence on the part of the newspaper was, according to King, due to the nature of some of Hugo's poems which *La Quotidienne* considered definitely out of step with its own ideas and doctrines.[13] On September 29 of that same year, Mély-Janin published an article in which he tried to justify *La Quotidienne's* lack of enthusiasm.[14] He admired the poems in which Hugo showed the usual Royalist and Catholic spirit, but voiced regret with respect to the poems written in the spirit of the new movement and which denoted a break with the fixed forms of classical poetry as well as a break with the separation of the genres. These poems, it was felt, also lacked that impersonal tone, as well as the equilibrium and eternal beauty of classical poetry. In his condemnation of the bold and ornate style of some of Hugo's poems and the mixing of genres, Mély-Janin was primarily attacking the "genre frénétique which, he felt, was a menace to society, a sign of revolution and anarchy.

Nodier, after having written his articles on Scott in which he defended not only Scott but Romanticism as well, wrote eight important articles in 1823 in which he defended and praised what he considered "good" Romanticism. Of those eight articles, the one he wrote on *Han d'Islande* is undoubtedly the most important in his relationship with Hugo. This article, written on March 12, 1823, for *La Quotidienne* is important for a number of reasons. First, because it appeared in the pages of a reactionary newspaper that had repeatedly expressed its abhorrence for this type of literature. Secondly, because, in view of the reservations Nodier sometimes expressed with respect to the "genre frénétique," he, nonetheless, defended and even praised a novel that was deeply imbued with vampirism, Satanism, with bizarre and extravagant language and settings, a novel that was influenced by the gothic novel, Sade, Richardson, Rousseau and, last but not least, Nodier's *Smarra*. Han d'Islande, the hero-villain, is a vampire, a demon, a father who drinks the blood of his victims out of the skull of his own son, a son he begot when he raped the young peasant girl, Lucy, on her wedding night, although she was wed to another. Han d'Islande is also a brigand and an outlaw, though by no means generous and noble, who disseminates all kinds of destruction, not for riches, not for gold, not to instill the sense of nationalism and human dignity in the souls of men, but "for blood." Third, because it established more firmly the relationship between Nodier and Hugo that was to continue for the next four or five years.

What Nodier praises in this novel is Hugo's erudition, his vivid and picturesque style, his delicacy of sentiments, traits he finds astonishing in so young a writer.[15] But, Nodier continues, why did such a fine talent feel it necessary to introduce certain extravagances and horrors with which this work is permeated? Nodier has an explanation: it is the youthfulness and impatience of the writer that is to blame. He then goes on to explain that the "genre frénétique" is something that is inevitable, a symptom of the age, expressing despair, anguish, fear,[16] traits that are totally different from either Greek Antiquity or the French classical period with their sense of propriety, equilibrium, and of muted sensations. Literature, says Nodier once more, is, after all, an expression of the age, an expression of the terrible convulsions that society is experiencing. He then concludes, almost despite himself, and somewhat maliciously, that

Romanticists, in general, are really not a bad lot, and one will do well not to accept either their ghouls or their vampires, although this type of revolting monster is not less hideous in Homer than in the imitators of Byron. But the faults of Homer are a privilege; besides, did it never occur to the bosses of the classical genre that ghouls and vampires were invented by Homer? [17]

The fact that ghouls, vampires, and werewolves were already present in the works of Homer and other classical writers will be stressed by Nodier once again in an article written on March 4, 1824 and again on December 22, 1825. In the article of 1825, Nodier writes that "there are ogres and vampires in the *Odyssey* . . . ghouls and werewolves in Apuleius. . . . Why does one consider the sorceresses in Ovid classical, but not so the witches of Shakespeare?" [18]

In his three articles dated January 12, March 19, and October 4 of 1823 (the latter one is devoted to Lamartine), Nodier declares once again that Romanticism is as moral as Classicism and that out of this new movement will emerge a new life that is fundamentally Christian. Rather than continue this paradoxical enslavement to "the sad monotony of Greek fables and the insipid boredom of polytheism," [19] the new movement will express ideas and sentiments that will make man dream and bring his soul in closer contact with his celestial origins. And, last but not least, Nodier says that Romanticism is Royalist to the core. The names of a Hugo, a Lamartine, a Vigny suffice to make this obvious. On June 4, 1823 Nodier repeats that Romanticism is the most recent and the most popular literature of the day, a view expressed by Stendhal in *Racine et Shakespeare* and *Beaudelaire* in *Curiosités esthétiques*. With his usual irony, Nodier writes that "we will always do homage to the purity of taste of the Aristotelian school, to the extent of its erudition and wisdom of its doctrines. But we will cry at the tragedies of the Romanticists." [20]

On March 8, 1824 Hugo published his *Nouvelles Odes,* and Nodier praised, with much perception, the literary values and beauty of these poems.[21] A note from Hugo, thanking Nodier for the kind things said in the article, indicates clearly that Nodier was still enthusiastic about the work of the younger man. However, what is rather strange about Nodier's article of March 8 is that the usual comments about Romanticism, the usual verve and frequent caustic humor, were gone. Indeed, something had happened which had nothing to do with Hugo. A war was on, a war on several fronts, declared by the editors of *La Quotidienne* on Romanticism. A war was also on between Mély-Janin and Nodier. In 1824 there is also evidence that *La Muse Française* began to defend Romanticism with renewed vigor and attacked these "Messieurs les Classiques" at *La Quotidienne.*[22] The year 1824 is also the year when Nodier ceased to collaborate so closely with *La Quotidienne* and accepted a post as librarian at the Arsenal. His article of March 4, 1824 is a reply to Mély-Janin's earlier attack and summarizes succinctly Nodier's basic ideas of the new literature. Romanticism, says Nodier, is a combination of "the literary beauty of the ancients, or rather of all ages, with the necessary modifications which changes in religion, institutions, traditions, localities must bring to composition and style." [23] Nonetheless, despite these feuds between Nodier and *La Quotidienne*, Nodier continued to write a few noncommittal articles for the newspaper. On February 10, 1827, Nodier wrote an article for *La Quotidienne* on the occasion of the recent publication of Hugo's *Odes et Ballades* where he speaks of "the delightful ballads in which the poet proves so well the astonishing flexibility of his talent, a talent which lends itself so easily to all the *genres* and that he has songs for the most delicate sentiments as well as for the most solemn thoughts." [24] But by this time, Nodier is tired of all the political intrigues associated with newspapers. In a letter to Weiss dated March 28, 1827, he says that he is sick of "the contradictory lies of *La Quotidienne* which says something is white and the *Constitutionnel*, which says something is red; and all the little rags of all shades." [25] We know also that by this time other personal matters began to affect Nodier, one of which was his relationship with Hugo.

After having written in February, 1827, a second favorable article on Hugo, Nodier, from now on, maintains a frozen silence with respect to the works that Hugo will publish. The year 1827 is, after all, the year when many of the habitués of the Arsenal move to the Cénacle held at the home of the Hugos; it is also the year when Hugo reads the five acts of his *Cromwell* to Sainte-Beuve and the former habitués of the Arsenal and when he is writing his *Préface de Cromwell*. According to an article by N. Wilson, entitled "Charles Nodier, Victor Hugo et *Les Feuilles d'automne*," it was Napoleon, *Cromwell*, and *Hernani* that weakened the relationship between Nodier and Hugo. Indeed, when one considers the intense dislike and fear Nodier had with respect to "totalitarian democracy," universal education, progress, and perfectibility, one can well understand why Nodier remained silent with respect to the presentation and publication of *Cromwell*. Furthermore, the Romanticism that Hugo now proclaimed was "liberalism in literature" as well as liberalism in politics and society; it was a Romanticism that had faith in the "loud and power-

ful voice of the people," and in the "literature of the people," [26] a
Romanticism that had little to do with the Romanticism of
Nodier. Art, for Hugo, was to be a tribune for the masses and a
means for expounding revolutionary ideas. Although he remained
silent between 1827 and 1830 with respect to the publication of
Hugo's works, Nodier, nonetheless, attacked him indirectly in an
article he wrote for *La Quotidienne* on November 1, 1829, entitled
*Byron et Moore,* which appeared shortly after the publication of
Hugo's *Orientales.* In this article Nodier's discussion of local color
as used discreetly by Scott, Byron, and Moore became an oblique
attack against Hugo's use of extravagant and dazzling colors and
exotic names in *Les Orientales.* "Indeed," says Nodier, "our
orientalists, if they have produced anything, have not yet composed a poem that comes close to the admirable compositions of
those great geniuses." [27] According to Schenck and Wilson, Hugo
was deeply hurt by Nodier's remarks which he realized were
aimed at him. In a letter to Nodier, Hugo cries out with:

And you too, Charles! I would give anything not to have read yester-
day's *La Quotidienne,* for one of life's most violent shocks is the one
that roots out from the heart an old and deep-seated friendship. . . .
Little by little, from silence and indifference toward me, I have seen
you pass to praise, enthusiasm, and acclaim for my enemies. . . . And
what a time for you to have chosen to attack! Just when my enemies
are railing against me from all sides. . . .[28]

It should be pointed out that this was the year when Hugo's
play, *Marion Delorme,* had been prevented from being performed
by a governmental interdiction, and that Hugo felt hounded from
all sides. It should also be noted that Nodier remained markedly
silent with respect to the publication of *Hernani* in 1830, all the
more astonishing since the play dealt with a theme very familiar
to Nodier, namely, the generous and noble outlaw. But Hugo's
outlaw is now disseminating revolution and urging a populace to
revolt against the established order and not, as in *Jean Sbogar,*
fighting against a foreign imperial power. Nevertheless, the year
1831 does, indeed, bring about a rapprochement between the two
men. Nodier, according to Wilson, indicated to Hugo that he
would lend his support to *Marion Delorme* and, to the great joy of
Hugo, "a somewhat prickly olive branch of peace and reconcilia-

tion appeared in *Le Temps* (31 October and 2 November 1831)." [29] In these articles Nodier, quite obviously, expresses more admiration for Hugo the poet than for Hugo the dramatist. One of the most important points that Nodier makes here is the idea that the dramatist should remain invisible; this is the exact opposite of what Hugo had stated in his *Préface de Cromwell.* Much of what Nodier says in these articles is nothing more than a sort of guide to a young dramatist who has shown considerable talent but who has gone wrong somewhere along the line. Although Hugo keenly sensed between the lines Nodier's attacks against his plays, he was, nevertheless, grateful to Nodier for having at least lent his support by merely writing about the play. For this support, Wilson says, Hugo prepared *Les Feuilles d'automne,* "a work after Nodier's own heart: a volume of pure poetry, autumn leaves unruffled by the political storms of the day and quietly adorning the eternal fleur de lys." [30] But Hugo is now caught between two opposing forces, a conflict that was difficult to resolve: to say kind and moderate things about the monarchy on the one hand, and his own revolutionary bias, on the other. In December, 1831, Nodier published his review of *Les Feuilles d'automne* in the pages of the *Revue de Paris.* Nodier praised the poetic values of this work, liking above all the personal statements of the poet, which he referred to as "meditations worthy of man." The place of the poet, Nodier says, should be high up in a tower above the multitudes, with Orpheus and Pythagoras, singing about "the perpetual harmony of the stars in their eternity." [31] The last paragraph of the article is a reminder that he, after all, had discovered Hugo's "rising glory" and that he is proud to have seen two young talents, that of Hugo and Lamartine, "born for the delight of future ages," [32] rise to their rightful place in heaven.

Given the temperament of the two men, it is understandable that the friendship between Nodier and Hugo could not last. Although both men, each in his own way, were ambitious, Hugo was undoubtedly the more aggressive of the two, as well as the more successful. It was also predictable that the support and appreciation that each of the two men had of the new Romantic movement could not be the same for long. Both did, indeed, start out as supporters of monarchy, Catholicism, and chivalry; both did, indeed, harbor the desire to give to France a new literature immersed in its own colorful past and imbued with its own tradi-

tions and values. Both said and felt this, but their basic premises
were different: Nodier was saying this as a critic of literature and
history; Hugo as an author who hoped to be one of the leaders of
the new movement. When around 1830 Romanticism culminated
into the militant Romanticism of Hugo, Nodier, strongly affected
by the Revolutions that were taking hold of all of Europe in 1830
and, disappointed at the trend Romanticism was taking, retired
from all the polemics of the day and turned more and more to a
world of his own making, the world of *Le Roi de Bohême* and *La
Fée aux miettes*. It should always be remembered that Nodier had
supported Romanticism primarily because he felt that Romanticism alone could give free reign to the imagination, the dream, as
well as to the fantastic and the marvelous.

## IV  *Nodier and Shakespeare*

When one compares the articles Nodier wrote on Hugo with
those he wrote on Shakespeare, one detects a noticeable difference. Whereas Nodier showed an increasingly marked aloofness,
even hostility, with respect to the work of Hugo, his admiration
and enthusiasm for Shakespeare never subsided. What was perhaps merely a sense of loyalty and duty toward Hugo and the new
movement was undeniably a feeling of love and kinship for what
he considered one of the greatest geniuses of all times. The hesitations and restraints that one discerns in his essays and comments
on Shakespeare, at least between the years 1801 and 1817, ema-
nate primarily from his reluctance to break away completely from
the traditional attitudes and beliefs of most of his compatriots.
When he finally does succeed in casting aside all reservations and
hesitations, his enthusiasm and praise for the English bard are
unbounded.

It is well known that the name of Shakespeare has been both
revered and vilified in France already in the eighteenth century.
Voltaire, for one, admired Shakespeare for his great and free spirit
but, Neoclassicist that he was, at least in literature, he was unable
to accept the Englishman's violations of the classical rules and the
mixing of the comic and the tragic. This restricted and restricting
attitude continued in France well into the nineteenth century, by
conservatives as well as by liberals (when on July 31, 1827, an
English troop performed *Othello* in English on the stage in Paris,
the actors were booed by liberals), for in the eyes of many

Frenchmen, England was often regarded as the cause for many of France's ills, social, political, as well as ideological. It comes as a surprise to discover that conservative newspapers during the first decades of the nineteenth century sound very much like their archfiend, Voltaire. When on January 11, 1815 Ducis adapted and presented *Hamlet* on the stage of the Comédie Française, the usual criticisms were leveled against the play: violation of the classical unities, the mixing of the sublime and the grotesque, the two appearances of the ghost of Hamlet's father, the use of crude and coarse language such as "something is rotten" and "I smell a rat." The French shuddered with horror and disgust at the thought that Mme de Staël could prefer such an atrocity as *Hamlet* to *Cinna* and *Phèdre*. They found Shakespeare barbaric and crude, and their fine sensibilities were offended at the sight of murders, duels, and battles. In view of this general attitude, it is interesting to note that Martainville, writing for the *Journal de Paris* on January 11, 1815, said the following with respect to Hamlet:

Hamlet is one of the most bizarre conceptions of the greatest genius England has produced, and if I did not fear to be stoned by my compatriots, I would even say that he was the most astonishing genius that has existed at all times. I will not give up trying to make more acceptable a heresy which revolts the haughty purity of a national cult. . . . Hamlet is mad, but what a sublime and sacred madness is the madness of a mind that has wandered because of the pain it feels by the death of a beloved father and the desire to avenge his ashes. Is not such a man holy who is mad out of filial piety? Where did Shakespeare find the idea for such a character? He cannot be found in any classical poets—he did not know them, and even if he had known them, they would not have been able to furnish him with even the model of the tiniest grain for such an audacious conception. It is in his head and in his heart that he discovered it.[33]

However, writing a few months later for the conservative *La Quotidienne*, Martainville was more subdued in his appreciation of the performance. Although he still admired Ducis' presentation of *Hamlet*, Martainville praised Ducis for having been discreet and "cleaned up" the play for French sensibilities. Nevertheless, he regretted the fact that Ducis had omitted from the play the scene in which Ophelia becomes mad; he admitted, though, that "we could not have tolerated her madness, although our neighbors are not wrong in finding the scene touching and dramatic." [34] Changes of this sort occurred frequently on the French stage. When an English troupe played at the Beaux-Arts between September, 1827, and June, 1828, the actors, aware of the sensibilities of the French public, shortened considerably the role of the madman in *King Lear*. (What they said about Edgar, son of Gloster, dressed and behaving like a madman, and the blinding of Gloster on the stage, is not known.) J. B. A. Soulié, drama critic at the time for *La Quotidienne,* although he appreciated the mixture of the sublime and the grotesque in *King Lear,* nevertheless, when it came to the presentation of *Romeo and Juliet,* found that the actress who played the role of Juliet was somewhat too realistic when she played the death scene. "It is only at the Theatre of the Boulevard that such dramatic perfection is tolerated," [35] he added. When Ducis presented *Othello,* the role of Iago was completely eliminated in order to spare the feelings of the French public.

Nodier, as we have seen, published his *Pensées de Shakespeare, extraits de ses ouvrages* already in 1801. This little volume consisted primarily of one hundred and ninety apothegms taken from a number of Shakespeare's plays. Important as this choice may appear—a choice that, according to critics, seems to have been geared primarily for moral edification rather than based on esthetic judgment—more important is Nodier's "Préliminaires" of less than five pages which reveals already his appreciation of the genius of Shakespeare. However, at that early date, Nodier does not basically differ greatly from the appraisal of the majority of his countrymen. For in these "Préliminaries," as well as in the articles he wrote for the *Journal des Débats* in 1814, Nodier, although never ceasing to admire Shakespeare's genius, says that he can see quite clearly the faults of the playwright. These "faults" are, of course, Shakespeare's violations of the classical rules, especially the mixing of the genres. On March 4, 1814, writing once again in the pages of the *Journal des Débats,* Nodier says that he prefers Aeschylus to Shakespeare's *Macbeth, Hamlet,* or *Richard III,* but that Shakespeare is better than Euripides in his portrayal of the misfortunes of Juliet and the despair of Ophelia; this is so because Shakespeare, in those instances, "has become classical and one can only regret that he has not always been so." [36] When on June 13, 1814 Nodier reviewed *Anthony and Cleopatra,* which had been presented as a ballet, he expresses an ambiguity in his appraisal of the buffoon in the play who, in this French version, no longer appeared grotesque. Nodier inclines to agree with this elimination of the grotesque which "the English find very pleasing and which our author did not dare to present in the original out of respect for what we consider good taste." [37] Yet, Nodier is quick to add, this was after all a ballet to which the classical rules are not applicable, thereby giving us the impression that he would have preferred Shakespeare's original interpretation. One is left with the distinct feeling that Nodier is trying everything within his power to prevent Shakespeare from being judged by the restricting standards of the classical rules. However, on May 14, 1814, in his discussion of Ducis' *Hamlet* for the *Journal des Débats*, Nodier's reservations are once more evident: "I am not an ardent admirer of Shakespeare; I attach great importance to his genius without being completely blinded to his faults; I am far from recommending his type of plays to our poets who have had the good fortune of having their talent formed by Euripides and Racine." [38]

Thus we find Nodier in 1814 (and even as late as 1817) playing the game of having to defend the classical rules while at the same time drawn toward the genius of Shakespeare and compelled to express this admiration. The problem for Nodier was how to reconcile the tastes and attitudes of the times with his own personal inclination and bias; more importantly, how was he to reconcile the genius of Shakespeare and his violations of the classical rules. According to O. G. Brockett, Nodier accomplished this feat by

locating a common denominator for the three [Shakespearian drama, melodrama, and Romantic drama] in melodrama, a new form for which no canons of taste had been established. By removing Shakespeare's work from the category of tragedy, Nodier was then able to admire it, even on the stage. . . . As such [the plays] could be regarded in the same light as the popular drama of the unsophisticated Boulevard theatres. [39]

Indeed, by regarding Shakespeare's plays as melodramas, Nodier was free to admire and praise Shakespeare without feeling the need to admonish him for his violations. This association on the part of Nodier of Shakespeare's plays with the Théâtre du Boulevard is considered somewhat sacrilegious by Brockett. Even

more distasteful to him is the fact that Nodier compared Shakespeare with Guilbert de Pixérécourt, "le roi du mélodrame." [40] Placing Shakespeare's plays in the category of melodramas and linking
his name with that of Pixérécourt is, according to Brockett, proof
that Nodier never really understood the poetic genius of Shakespeare and merely sought in his plays moral instruction and edification. This may, in part, be true of Nodier, especially the early
Nodier who did, indeed, see in Romanticism the development of a
new national literature which would give back to France the old
moral and religious virtues. But moral instruction was by no
means the sole reason for Nodier's admiration of Shakespeare.
Nodier did, indeed, place the plays of Shakespeare into the same
category as melodrama; but his reason for doing so seems to be
misinterpreted by Brockett. Nodier did so primarily to avoid
having to condemn Shakespeare for violating the classical rules,
especially at a time when Romanticism, in 1814, was still speaking, at least in France, in a weak and muted voice. If Brockett had
checked some of Nodier's later comments on the foreign theater,
he would have discovered that Nodier, in an article entitled *Chefs-
d'oeuvre des théâtres étrangers,* dated December 4, 1822, and
written for *La Quotidienne,* took the Classicists to task for accus-
ing the Romanticists of imitating and admiring foreign literature.
Classicists, Nodier notes, are eager to condemn Romanticists for
using foreign literatures and styles; but, he adds, somewhat maliciously, have not the classical dramatists, from Mairet and Corneille on, admired and imitated foreign literature? And he cites
especially the influence of Spanish and Italian literature on
France.[41]

In his essay entitled *Des Types en littérature* (1830), Nodier
says that "Shakespeare is as rich in his presentation of *types* as
was Homer, and was able to discover them in all the levels of
the imagination, from the most natural and positive to the most
delirious fantasy." [42] In these types Nodier includes Mercutio,
Othello, Puck, Caliban, and the "sublime" Hamlet, that prototype of the Middle Ages.[43] By types Nodier does not mean the one-
dimensional characters of, say, Gil Blas or the *Commedia dell' Arte;*
rather, by types in literature, Nodier is referring to those characters whose "proper names have almost become substantives in all
languages," and who have become "the representative sign of a
conception, a creation, an idea." [44] This is quite apparent, says

Nodier, in such names as Werther and René. And it is this ability to create types and to infuse the characters with an original individuality which eventually becomes so familiar to one that is the mark of genius. This is precisely why such writers as Shakespeare, Rabelais, the "Homère Bouffon de France," [45] and Cervantes are geniuses. France does not have too many of these types. "What France lacked," says Nodier, "was the literary freedom so vehemently contested ever since there was a literature, all in the name of Aristotle, the Sorbonne, the University, the Academy and which . . . undoubtedly will be refused her today in the name of liberty." [46] The English, Nodier feels, have been freer to create types and, above all, they have been able to develop a state of mind and an atmosphere that is conducive to the development of such types.

That Nodier greatly admired Shakespeare no one, not even Brockett, will gainsay. The question, then, centers around the source of Nodier's admiration. What did Nodier admire in Shakespeare? Was it simply the moral teachings that quite naturally emerge from the plays of Shakespeare? When one takes Nodier's own creative work into consideration, his fiction as well as his critical essays, one soon becomes convinced that Nodier admired and loved those writers who possessed great and powerful imaginations, writers who were able to have gigantic dreams and visions. And it is for that reason that he admired such writers as Shakespeare, Homer, Dante, Rabelais, and Laurence Sterne. What Nodier admired in Shakespeare was his ability to dream, to create new worlds, and the expression of the fantastic and the marvelous in his works. This can be seen in his article of 1821 when, writing for *La Foudre* in connection with Guizot's edition of Shakespeare, he says that Shakespeare's genius "was as enormous as nature itself, as unequal, as admirable, and even as monstrous as nature. Everything is real in Shakespeare and the magical world takes on in his hands an exquisite natural aspect." [47]

What Nodier has said about Shakespeare in his articles and reviews is certainly important and worthy of consideration. Equally important, however, is the influence Shakespeare has exerted on the works of Nodier. Many of the cherished characters found in the plays of Shakespeare have appeared, in modified form, in the tales of Nodier. It is not by accident that two of the most delightful characters emerging from the imagination of Shakespeare would also appeal to the imagination of Nodier: Puck and Ariel. Already on February 4, 1814 in the *Journal des Débats*, in a discussion of Slavic literature, Nodier talks about "the nocturnal concerts of Puck, Ariel, and all the little goblins of Shakespeare when, newly emerged from their flowers and still damp with dew, they sing songs unknown to human ears." [48] It is obvious that Nodier patterned his little will-o'-the-wisp, Trilby, after Puck and Ariel, for, in many ways, Trilby combines the spritelike quality of Puck with the more human, and thus more tragic, quality of Ariel. Trilby is Puck when he is the little house spirit, irresponsible and malicious, performing domestic duties for pretty maidens, while playing malicious pranks upon the old slatterns. Like Puck, he is perhaps only a midsummer night's dream, born of the idleness and suppressed desires of a Jeannie. But Trilby is also Ariel when he loves Jeannie and becomes human and therefore vulnerable. Trilby, imprisoned in an oak tree for one thousand years by the monk Ronold, is a fellow sufferer of Ariel who was also imprisoned in a tree by a witch until Prospero set him free. Nodier also expressed interest in the character of Caliban who, he feels, represents the other side of man's dual nature, what he called "la bête fauve" in man, that is, man's material nature, as opposed to man's spiritual nature, represented by Ariel.

The world Nodier loves in Shakespeare is, of course, the magic fairyland so familiar in English literature and legend, a world which, Nodier felt, still existed in many parts of nineteenth-century England and Scotland and which he tried to capture in *Trilby*. This magical world of spirits, witches, sorcerers, the world of the supernatural, the mysterious and the marvelous, had also existed in France during the Middle Ages, a world which he felt still lay dormant within the ruins of France, ready to come to life once again through the creative adventure of its writers. Nodier, with Taylor and Cailleux, was the first to introduce the French public to the gothic monuments of France. In 1800 the three men published their impressions of their trip through historic France in a work entitled *Voyages pittoresques et romantiques dans l'ancienne France,* thereby making the link between the Middle Ages and Romanticism. For Nodier wished to restore to France her ancient marvels and legends. [49]

It is interesting to compare Nodier's belief in the world of the supernatural and the preternatural with that of Shakespeare.

Shakespeare, although he no longer believed in the lore and legends, the beliefs and superstitions of his day, nonetheless, as a
thoroughgoing man of the Renaissance, took all the phenomena
available to him: the supernatural and preternatural, the natural
history of the *Book of Beasts,* as well as his own experience and
observations. These supernatural elements usually served him as
episodes and provided devices for intensifying an already strange
and weird atmosphere; their main function was to thrill the audi-
ence. Thus, Shakespeare, like many of the Elizabethan dramatists
and the writers of gothic novels, used these devices to enhance
their poetic craft. Nodier, too, used these phenomena to create an
atmosphere and enhance his poetic craft. It would appear,
though, that Nodier, perhaps more than Shakespeare, wanted
desperately to believe in an enchanted and enchanting world. Living in an age of skepticism and disillusionment, he wanted to
believe in the world of Puck and Ariel; he needed to walk with
Trilby at his side along the banks of the Clyde. Nodier, in his *Du
Fantastique dans la littérature,* says that the fantastic, which he
equates with the imagination, the ability to dream, appears in literature when belief in religion, magic, ghosts, goblins, fairies and
vampires, has long disappeared. It is then that these beliefs, legends, and myths appear in fiction and are presented in a tale in
which one pretends to believe or desperately wants to believe.
Literature, continues Nodier in this same essay, became fantastic
when it invented the lie, that is, when it began to dream. This has
been the case throughout the history of literature. In fact, says
Nodier, even religion has depended upon the fantastic in its creation of myths. And it is this very special element, the fantastic and
the marvelous, that distinguishes great works of art from second-
ary works. It is this very quality in the works of Shakespeare that
made Nodier love and revere, as well as imitate, the world created
by Shakespeare.

# CHAPTER 9

# *Conclusion*

CHARLES NODIER, as this study attempts to demonstrate, can and should be considered as an important precursor of the Romantic movement, who, already around 1800, initiated and supported the new movement at a time when Romanticism was still speaking, at least in France, with a weak and muted voice. Nodier, more perhaps than other French Romanticists, was extremely susceptible to the ideas that were penetrating into France from across the Rhine and the Channel. This is especially true with respect to Nodier's comprehension and interpretation of German Romanticism with its stress on the dream and the fantastic and their impact on the psychic life of man and their use in literature. Although Romanticism was a revolt against Cartesianism, rationalism, logic, and Classicism, Romanticism also stood for the free play of the imagination. It is in this respect that Nodier can be considered, if not the inventor, at least the initiator of the *conte fantastique* in France, for the imagination and the dream, both nocturnal and diurnal, play an important role in this genre. The *conte fantastique* (and herein lies its essential difference from the ordinary *conte*) gives unprecedented prominence to the *vie intérieure*—the most important part of the *double vie*, as Asselineau called the reality/dream dichotomy. The *conte fantastique* attempts to reproduce the nightmarish quality of the dream with its disregard for coherence, time, space, and sequence; it is steeped in a sense of morbidity and aims at achieving a "frisson de l'épouvante" and at penetrating the unknown. Often, under the superficial cloak of the burlesque or the grotesque and the occasional introduction of ghosts, vampires, werewolves, and phantoms, one always feels present in these writings an undercurrent of the supernatural or the occult; equally present is a basic tone of despair, fear, anguish, and revolt (personal or metaphysical) which expresses, directly or indirectly, the obsession of an age as

156

well as the personal obsessions of the individual author. In general, it is the *fantastique intérieure,* the psychologically oriented fantastic, principally introduced by E. T. A. Hoffmann, that is at work in the *conte fantastique* of Nodier. It is thanks to Nodier, primarily through his familiarity with German Romanticism, that French Romanticism was given a deeper and more psychologically and philosophically oriented significance.

The tremendous enthusiasm found in Nodier as well as in other French and German Romanticists for the world of the imagination, the dream, the fantastic and the marvelous, their attempt to escape into a world of their own creation, the elimination of space and time was also shared with no less enthusiasm by many Surrealists. In many respects, Nodier's attempt to escape into a world of the imagination, the dream, and infuse the world of everyday existence with the fantastic and the marvelous, is equally apparent in the literature of escape in the post-World War I period. After the end of World War I, symptoms similar to those of the *mal du siècle* of the Romantic period were once more in evidence. When four years of bloodletting, of havoc, and misery, were over, relief overtook the victors as well as the vanquished. The immediate reaction was one of euphoria, for people were under the assumption that the delayed millennium could now at last be attained. This euphoric state is expressed vividly in the term "les années folles," which began on November 12, 1918 with the Première of *Phi-Phi,*[1] an operetta whose success was enormous throughout the world. So great was the optimism immediately after World War I, so easily were success and fortune achieved, that, to some, the utopian society could now be attempted with even greater hope of success. World War I had, after all, been fought to end all wars, to make the world safe for democracy, honor, justice, and all the other noble and cherished abstractions.

But when the big parade was over, when the bright floodlights were turned off and the pale light of morning began to appear, it soon began to be apparent that all the war had brought with it was an attempt to simulate the facile optimism that had existed during the period called "la belle époque," that is, the pre-World War I period. The much-awaited millennium was nowhere in sight. With the "return to normalcy" came the disillusionment and pessimism of the more thoughtful and sensitive who looked about themselves and realized that they had been cheated and that democracy had never really been the concern of the men who made decisions about war and peace. What they called "democracy" was nothing more than economic rights and privileges. What they saw was that the Johnnies who had got their guns had also come home as basket cases.

With the World War I period, one witnesses the actual breakdown of a world which, for many decades, had held together by no real values but by sheer force of habit, inertia, and convenience. A sense of bitterness and frustration, and even nihilism, coupled with a sense of rootlessness and defeatism, engendered in the sensitive individual a desire to escape into a world totally different from the one that their elders had passed on to them. Thus a revolt against the social, political, and religious order once more took place as it had done during the period of Romanticism. As before, it was a revolt against rationalism and order, against the intellect as well as against literature and language. The facile optimism of Anatole France and the nationalism of Maurice Barrès were anathema to the modern Romanticists. The Surrealists, and their precursors the Dadaists, reacted as violently against the times as had the Romanticists in their own time. Like the Romanticists, the Surrealists wished to escape from the outmoded and hypocritical strictures of society, to break away from a reality that had no meaning. Revolt for the Surrealists meant a liberation from all restraints. It was moral in the sense that it was a refusal to conform to certain ideas and beliefs, certain modes of life which they considered invalid. But their revolt was also a metaphysical revolt in that it was a revolt against the human condition, against those inexorable forces which combine to crush man.

Like Nodier, Nerval, Gautier, Baudelaire, Rimbaud, Lautréamont, and many other writers of the nineteenth century, the Surrealists were also attracted and repelled by the veritgo they experienced when confronted with the *néant* as well as with the infinite. They, too, hoped to find in death something new, an answer to the enigma. Fear of and fascination with death and attempts at suicide were not uncommon in the 1920's as had been the case among Romanticists—in their own lives as well as in their works. Jacques Vaché, found dead with a companion, had, according to Breton, committed suicide. To choose the time and the place of one's death is an attempt to revolt against the human condition. In *Lettres de guerre*, Vaché is quite explicit in stressing the decision to commit suicide rather than the act itself. "I object to being killed in war. . . . I shall die when I want to die, and then I shall die with somebody else. To die alone is boring. . . . I should prefer to die with one of my best friends." [2] Jacques Rigaut, after having tried to kill himself three times, finally succeeded in shooting himself in the heart. Rigaut, too, tries to explain his act, that is, the decision to commit suicide. His slim volume, entitled *Agence générale du suicide*, reveals his obsession with suicide.

The reaction of the Surrealists to men such as Barrès, France, and Paul Bourget was a reaction similar to the one experienced by the Romanticists against Voltaire, the *Philosophes, Idéologues,* and Classicism. In both cases it was a reaction against the tyranny of reason and logic, against a facile optimism and a messianic approach toward art. Nodier, like so many Romanticists, and like the Surrealists, favored the unconscious, the intuitive or irrational aspects of man's nature. Nodier as well as the Surrealists extolled the dream as expressing this hidden, suppressed, and, therefore, authentic side of man—a source of true knowledge. Both Nodier and the Surrealists considered the world of the dream as immeasurably superior to the one afforded them during their daily lives. Interest in the occult and in magic was converse to their interest in science and its connection with order and reason. Science, with its positivistic approach, was excluded from consideration and held in complete disdain by Nodier and many Romanticists, as well as by many Surrealists. All preferred the *voyant,* the creator of visions and dreams, to the *savant.*

Parallels can also be made between Nodier and the Surrealists not only in their consideration of the world of the imagination, the dream as being vastly superior to the world of reality; they can also be made in their attitude toward time. Time, the great restrictionist and destroyer, was no more tolerated by the Surrealists than it was by Nodier, Gautier, Nerval, or Baudelaire. Like the Romanticists, the Surrealists were well aware that the world of the dream was an excellent liberator from space and time. For to escape from the world of physical reality into a world of the dream was also at the basis of Surrealism. In his *Manifeste* of 1924, André Breton reveals the importance he attributes to the world of the dream: "I believe in the future resolution of these two states, dream and reality, which are seemingly so contradictory, into a kind of absolute reality, a *surreality,* if one may so speak. It is in quest of this surreality that I am going." [3]

Because the world of the child is also that of the world of the imagination, the dream, the Surrealists like to return to that *paradis primitif* of Nodier, Baudelaire, Nerval, and Rimbaud. Children, like madmen and fools, are frequently portrayed by the Surrealists. Those "innocents," as Nodier called them, possess the gift of voyance and have direct knowledge of another world, the world on the other side of the looking glass. *Les enfants terribles,* Thomas l'Imposteur, Nadja, Vitrac's Victor, like Michel, Jean-François les Bas-Bleus, or Xaïloun, are especially sensitive to the world of the dream and escape into a world of their own creation, a world with its own sense of order and logic, its own rules. Cocteau, like Nodier, forever retained a childlike innocence and faith in the world of magic and the dream.

Certain surrealistic qualities found in the dream as well as a form of automatic writing are also visible in the works of certain French Romanticists. Both Nodier and Nerval, for instance, made conscious attempts at reproducing these qualities in some of their works. In *Les Pas perdus,* Breton speaks of "a certain psychic automatism which corresponds easily to the state of the dream, a state which is extremely difficult today to define." [4] This "état de rêve" to which Breton alludes is precisely the "état de rêverie supernaturaliste" to which Nerval alludes in his discussion and justification of his poem *El Desdichado.*[5] This "état de rêve" with its trancelike qualities is also quite apparent in certain works of Nodier. *Smarra,* as already noted, contains those disorderly, incoherent, and digressive qualities that are associated with the dream and with Surrealism. It is these qualities, so modern in their technique, that disturbed and confused many of Nodier's contemporaries. In his *Préface nouvelle* to *Smarra,* Nodier says:

It has been judged that the tale was not clear; that at the end of a reading one was left with a vague and even inextricable idea; that the mind of the narrator, continuously distracted by the most fugitive details, lost himself in every instance in digressions without purpose; that the transitions in the tale were never determined by the natural relationship of the thought, *junctura mixturaque,* but, rather, seemed to be abandoned to the capricousness of the word, left to chance, as in a game of dice; that in the final analysis, it was impossible to discern a rational plan and a stated goal.[6]

The notion of the association of ideas is indirectly suggested by Nodier in his discussion of the technique used in *Smarra:* "The most difficult strategem of the poet is of having enclosed the tale with a well-sustained anecdote which has an exposition, an end, *peripeteia* and a dénouement in a succession of bizarre dreams whose transition is often determined merely by a word." [7] In *Souvenirs de la Révolution,* Nodier again alludes to this unusual method which conveys the irregular, the haphazard, and the free association of ideas:

The title *Souvenirs* explains everything. Indeed, it is in this manner that souvenirs present themselves to the memory, in an irregular, capricious, diverse manner, without order, without method, and even without design, like the perceptions of sleep . . .

In the abandonment of a conversation which errs from subject to subject, or a tale which develops freely, at the pleasure of one's fancy, the imperceptible thread which ties ideas together has a usage that is totally different from that of Ariane's thread. It serves to pleasantly lead astray one's thought in a multitude of confused paths and does not allow it to find again the forgotten point from which it set out. One must break it and not follow it in order to emerge from the labyrinth.[8]

Ample use of digressions, association of ideas, abandonment, incoherence, is, of course, markedly apparent in *La plus petite des pantoufles* and, more importantly, in *Le Roi de Bohême.* In the latter work, Nodier attempts to reproduce the dream with its incoherence, its interruptions and digressions, its use of free association, the "dérèglement de tous les sens," the fusion of diverse realities, and the violation of space and time. The magic of words, their significance magnified by the use of sound, their position and arrangement on the page, the use of the oneiric pun, are also evident in this work. All these characteristics, usually associated with the Symbolists and, above all, the Surrealists, Nodier made use of already in 1805 and, more pronouncedly, around 1830. He can, for that reason, be considered a precursor of Freud and Surrealism.

All these characteristics, so evident in Nodier and in many Surrealists, are essentially an attack on reason, order, science, and physical reality. Rightly or wrongly, Nodier and many of his contemporaries, like the Surrealists, felt that reason had failed to provide the answers they sought; hence, their interest in the occult, secret societies, their enthusiasm for and travels to the Orient, and their experimentation with drugs. In their search for knowledge and salvation, in their attempt to make the invisible visible and the impalpable palpable, they soon discovered that travel, the occult, as well as drugs, were unsatisfactory and short-lived, and both the Romanticists and the Surrealists were astute enough to realize that the way to make the dream permanent, to get at the world behind the world of appearances, and to combat disintegration, time and space, was through the transformation of the dream into art.

Nodier, in the creation of his *conte fantastique*, provided himself with a theater of his own, one in which he could play different roles: the libertine in *L'Amour et le Grimoire* or *Moi-même*, Michel, young and pure of heart, Jeannie or Trilby, or both. These *contes* also provided Nodier with an area for expressing his ideas on the dream and its impact on man's psychic life. By means of this theater he has sometimes managed to make the unpleasant pleasant and the impossible possible. It has by now become apparent that Nodier particularly liked to project himself into the world of children who have not yet been corrupted by adults, or adults with childlike qualities, for childhood, one's own or an imaginary one, is also a place of refuge from an alien and menacing world. The child, like the dreamer or the madman, is a maker of worlds; for him, it is only this created world that is real; all else, the external world or reality, with its menacing adults, is merely the figment of the imagination. Like his innocents, Nodier believes in the world he has created for himself and for those who, like him, believe in the world of the dream, in the world of the fantastic and the marvelous. Sometimes, however, this world is filled with fear and anguish, sometimes terror, but Nodier was often able to transform this fear into irony. It is this sense of irony, the grotesque, and the creation of an autonomous world of the imagination that are important aspects of the fantastic. And it is through the very creation of an autonomous world where reason and nature are challenged that Nodier as well as his reader could achieve a sense of liberation.

Interest in the dream and the fantastic is not a new phenomenon. It is equally evident in the works of earlier writers—one has only to remember the works of Agrippa d'Aubigné, Cyrano de Bergerac, Rabelais, Restif de la Bretonne, Jacques Cazotte, to name but a few and limit oneself to one country—as well as in the 1820's and 1830's, and the 1920's and 1930's. Recent years have seen a resurgence of interest in the dream and the fantastic, as exemplified by reviews such as *Arcanes, Opus, L'Arc,* and the many recent publications by the publishing house of Eric Losfeld ( *Le Terrain Vague* ) and of José Corti. Corti has republished several gothic novels and many works of German Romanticists; Losfeld has devoted himself to republishing the works of Lautréamont, Benjamin Péret, and other Surrealists, as well as works on eroticism. Finally, witness the fact that the 1960's and 1970's are a period of disillusionment, protest, "dropping out," the happening, and psychedelic art. Witness also the rapport between Surrealism and student protest groups in France as well as in Germany and the United States. "L'Imagination au pouvoir" was, after all, the slogan of the Student Revolution of 1968.

Just as many Romanticists scorned the concepts of the *Philosophes* and the *Physiocrates* and their deification of reason, nature, and empiricism and turned to the occult and the Orient, just as in the 1920's the Surrealists scorned science and technology and all that was associated with the Occident and once again turned to the Orient and primitivism, so do we see signs of a similar trend pointing to an interest in the Orient and mysticism. Indeed, any trend toward rationalism and materialism brings about a counter-trend: the occult, mysticism, and illuminism. The fewer the people who avowedly believe, the bolder becomes the world of the dream and the intrusion of the fantastic and the marvelous. This seems to suggest that it serves as a protest against an ever-increasing materialism and rationalism. The nineteenth century became more and more steeped in the occult and the supernatural to counteract the industrial revolution and the revolutions of 1789, 1830, and 1848. Thus, all these political, social, and economic revolutions were producing what Toffler has called a "culture shock." The twentieth century, like the nineteenth century, is experiencing, perhaps even more vehemently, a culture shock of a similar nature. The enigmas of life and death, fear of the unknown, still haunt man, as they haunted man during the nineteenth century.

Disillusioned with the accomplishments of their age and, above all, with the accomplishments the age had promised them, skeptical of any new discoveries and pronouncements, man of the twentieth century, like man of the nineteenth century, turns to the occult sciences, magic, drugs, in order to find a paradise, real or artificial.

# Notes and References

## Preface

1. E. A. Poe, *Tales and Poems* (New York: The Viking Press, 1965), p. 95.

## Chapter One

1. This is the thesis of A. Cobban, *A History of Modern France* (Baltimore: Penguin, 1967).
2. Georg Brandes, *Revolution and Reaction in Nineteenth Century French Literature* (New York: Russell and Russell, n.d.).
3. Charles Nodier, *Contes* (Paris: Garnier, 1961), p. 720. The quotations of Nodier were translated by the author with the assistance of Françoise Demerson Baker. The texts of Nerval (other than the quotations taken from *Sylvie* and *Aurélia*), Charles Asselineau, Sainte-Beuve, Marcel Schneider, P. G. Castex, Albert Béguin, were translated by the author.
4. Nodier, *Contes*, p. 721.
5. Nodier, *Oeuvres complètes* (Geneva: Slatkine Reprints, 1968), IX, 249.
6. Gérard de Nerval, *Selected Writings* (Ann Arbor: University of Michigan Press, 1970), p. 50.
7. Nerval, *Selected Writings*, p. 157.
8. Alfred de Vigny, *Military Servitude and Grandeur* (New York: George H. Doran, 1919), p. 14.
9. Alfred de Musset, *The Confession of a Child of the Century* (New York: Privately printed and copyrighted by James L. Perkins and Co., 1908), pp. 12–13.
10. François-René de Chateaubriand, *Atala and René* (New York: Signet Classics, 1962), p. 120.
11. Nerval, *Oeuvres* (Paris: Pléiade, 1966), II, 92.
12. Elaine Marks, ed., *French Poetry from Baudelaire to the Present* (New York: Laurel Language Library, 1962), p. 69.
13. The best example of the "Romantic Agony" in Russian literature is Lermontov's *A Hero of Our Time*, whose hero Pechorin suffers from the same malady that had afflicted the Werthers, the Renés, the

*165*

Byrons, and the Adolphes. In Italy Giacomo Leopardi and Gabriele D'Annunzio, two dissimilar artists, living in different times of the nineteenth century, are, nevertheless, victims of the *mal du siècle*.

14. Carl Becker, *The Heavenly City of the 18th Century Philosophes* (New Haven: Yale University Press, 1959), p. 52.

15. Albert Béguin, *L'Ame romantique et le rêve* (Paris: Corti, 1963), p. 15.

16. Nietzsche's ideas on art and the dream parallel those of such writers as Nodier, Nerval, Baudelaire, and others (cf. *The Birth of Tragedy*). Nietzsche was an avid reader of Baudelaire.

17. Nerval, *Oeuvres*, I, 381.

18. Goethe, *Faust*, Part I (Middlesex: Penguin, 1949), p. 67.

19. Nodier, *Contes*, p. 168.

20. Charles Baudelaire, *Paris Spleen* (New York: New Directions, 1970), p. 49.

21. Nerval, *Oeuvres*, II, 12–13.

22. Nerval, *Oeuvres*, I, 950.

23. Béguin, *L'Ame romantique et le rêve*, p. 15.

24. Nodier, *Contes*, p. 39.

25. Nerval, *Selected Writings*, p. 115.

26. Charles Asselineau, *La Double Vie* (Paris: Poulet-Malassis et De Broise, 1858), pp. 171–72. Quoted also in Baudelaire, *Oeuvres complètes* (Paris: Pléiade, 1961), pp. 660–61.

27. Marcel Schneider, *La Littérature fantastique en France* (Paris: Fayard, 1964), p. 8.

28. Baudelaire, *Paris Spleen*, p. 33.

29. Walter Scott, *On Novelists and Fiction* (London: Routledge and Kegan Paul, 1968), p. 325.

30. P.-G. Castex, *Le Conte fantastique en France* (Paris: Corti, 1962), p. 48.

31. Sainte-Beuve, *Premiers Lundis* (Paris: Calmann Lévy, 1886), pp. 416–17.

## Chapter Two

1. Marcel Proust, *On Art and Literature* (New York: Delta Book, 1964), pp. 99–100.

2. Nodier, *Oeuvres complètes*, II, 278.

3. Léonce Pingaud, *La Jeunesse de Charles Nodier* (Besançon: Dodivers, 1914), p. 57.

4. Nodier, *Oeuvres complètes*, II, 140.

5. Carl Jung, *Memories, Dreams, Reflexions* (New York: Vintage, 1963), p. 189.

6. Nodier, *Contes*, p. 4.

7. H. Juin, *Charles Nodier* (Paris: Editions Pierre Seghers, 1970), p. 48.

8. Estignard, Alexandre, *Correspondance inédite de Charles Nodier* (Paris: Petiau, 1877), p. 20. Also quoted in Nodier, *Contes,* p. 4, the "Notice" by Castex.

9. Pingaud, p. 249.

10. Pingaud, p. 261.

11. Nodier, *Oeuvres complètes,* II, 32–33.

12. Nodier, *Oeuvres complètes,* II, 8.

13. Nodier, *Oeuvres complètes,* II, 9.

14. Nodier, *Oeuvres complètes,* II, 10.

15. Nodier, *Oeuvres complètes,* II, 20.

16. Goethe, *The Sorrows of Young Werther* (New York: Signet Classic, 1962), p. 109.

17. Goethe, *Werther,* p. 61.

18. Nodier, *Oeuvres complètes,* II, 96.

19. Nodier, *Contes,* p. 17.

20. Nodier, *Contes,* p. 17.

21. Nodier, *Contes,* p. 18.

22. Nodier, *Contes,* p. 20.

23. Nodier, *Oeuvres complètes,* II, pp. 128–29.

24. Nodier, *Contes,* p. 13.

25. Chateaubriand, *Atala and René,* p. 192.

26. Nodier, *Oeuvres complètes,* II, 134.

27. Nodier, *Oeuvres complètes,* II, 142.

28. Nodier, *Oeuvres complètes,* II, 354.

29. Nodier, *Oeuvres complètes,* IX, 289.

30. Nodier, *Oeuvres complètes,* IX, 299. See also Nodier's essay entitled *Réaction Thermidorienne,* VIII, 74.

### Chapter Three

1. Nodier, *Oeuvres complètes,* I, 7.

2. Nodier, *Oeuvres complètes,* I, 14.

3. Nodier, *Oeuvres complètes,* I, 34.

4. Rudolf Maixner, *Charles Nodier et l'Illyrie.* Études de littérature étrangère et comparée, No. 37 (Paris: Dider, 1960), p. 61.

5. Mario Praz, *The Romantic Agony* (New York: The World Publishing Co., 1963), p. 56.

6. Byron, *The Works* (London: Charles Scribner's, 1900), III, 237.

7. Maixner, p. 22.

8. Nodier, *Oeuvres complètes,* I, 134.

9. Nodier, *Oeuvres complètes,* I, 83.

10. Nodier, *Oeuvers complètes,* I, 56.

11. Nodier, *Oeuvres complètes*, I, 165.

12. Nodier, *Oeuvres complètes*, I, 165.

13. Nodier, *Oeuvres complètes*, I, 170.

14. Nodier, *Oeuvres complètes*, I, 23.

15. Maixner, pp. 61–62.

16. Nodier, *Oeuvres complètes*, I, 136.

17. The Tablettes of Lothario are reminiscent of the Tablets in Byron's *Corsair* which Conrad gives to his beloved before his departure and which also express "words of high trust and truth."

18. This and the following Tablettes are from *Jean Sbogar* (*Oeuvres complètes*, I, 241–59).

19. Nodier, *Oeuvres complètes*, I, 260.

20. Nodier, *Oeuvers complètes*, VI, 5.

21. Nodier, *Oeuvres complètes*, VIII, 132.

22. Nodier, *Oeuvres complètes*, VIII, 134.

23. Nodier, *Oeuvres complètes*, VIII, 135.

### Chapter Four

1. Mary Shelley, *Frankenstein or The Modern Prometheus* (New York, Collier Books, 1967), p. 8.

2. Schneider, p. 128. See also Voltaire, *Philosophical Dictionary* (New York: Basic Books, 1961), II, 453; *Encyclopédie* (Neufchastel: Samuel Faulche, 1765), XVI, 828. In both works Calmet and his "absurd works" are mentioned together with vampires.

3. Eunice Morgan Schenck, *La Part de Charles Nodier dans la formation des idées romantiques de Victor Hugo jusqu'à la préface de Cromwell* (Paris: Champion, 1914), p. 40.

4. Eunice Morgan Schenck, pp. 54–55.

5. Nodier, *Contes*, p. 34.

6. Nodier, *Contes*, p. 43.

7. Nodier, *Contes*, pp. 38–39.

8. Nodier, *Contes*, p. 61.

9. Nodier, *Contes*, p. 102.

10. Nodier, *Contes*, p. 105.

11. Nodier, *Contes*, p. 105.

12. Nodier, *Contes*, p. 105.

13. Nodier, *Contes*, p. 110.

14. Nodier, *Contes*, p. 111.

15. Nodier, *Contes*, p. 111.

16. Nodier, *Contes*, p. 89.

17. Nodier, *Contes*, pp. 99–100.

18. The word *mensonge* has been given an interesting interpretation by Nodier, as well as by Baudelaire and Asselineau. All three have equated the word with the imaginative faculty, the dream. Nodier, in

*Le Fantastique dans la littérature,* says that literature became fantastic when it "invented the lie." (*Oeuvres complètes,* V, 71.) In the same essay he points out that, as far as the public is concerned, "truth is merely a sophism, and virtue only a name" (p. 111) whereas "it is lies that amuse it." (p. 112). Baudelaire in *Semper Eadem* says: "Let, Oh let my heart become drunk with a *lie.*" In one of Asselineau's tales entitled *Le Mensonge,* the hero considers Corneille's *menteur* as his hero. After asking himself the question: "What is life?" Asselineau's hero concludes that life is a *mensonge;* and when asked: "What is a lie?" he replies: "Imagination to the second power." (According to W. T. Gairdner: *Un Ami de Baudelaire: Charles Asselineau, Sa Vie et son Oeuvre,* Paris, 1946, Asselineau's hero is patterned after Baudelaire who, it seemed, resembled Corneille's *menteur.*) Charles Mauron in *Le Dernier Baudelaire* (Paris: Corti, 1966) discusses Baudelaire's tendency to mystify and fool people with respect to his background and his life. The idea of the *mensonge* being equated with the imagination is again picked up by the Surrealists and sympathizers of Surrealism. Cocteau's radio monologue *Le Menteur* juxtaposes the words *mensonge* and *vérité.* He soon confuses the words and, in the end, opts for the former: "A lie," he says, "a lie, that's magnificent. Say . . . imagine an unreal world and make people believe—lie! It is true that truth weighs heavily and flabbergasts me. Truth. The two are of equal value. Perhaps the lie gets the better of it."

19. Nodier, *Contes,* p. 97.

### Chapter Five

1. Nodier, *Oeuvres complètes,* V, 161.
2. Nodier, *Oeuvres complètes,* V, 162.
3. Nodier, *Oeuvres complètes,* V, 180.
4. Nodier, *Oeuvres complètes,* V, 172–73.
5. Nodier, *Oeuvres complètes,* XI, 171. Nodier analyzes this state in his essay on *Piranèse, Contes psychologiques, à propos de la monomanie réflective.*
6. See footnote 18 of Chapter 4 for a discussion of the use of the word "lie."
7. Nodier, *Contes,* p. 719.
8. Nodier, *Contes,* p. 516.
9. Nodier, *Contes,* pp. 517–18.
10. Nodier, *Contes,* pp. 362–63.
11. Nodier, *Contes,* p. 170.
12. Nodier, *Contes,* p. 170.
13. Nodier, *Contes,* p. 38.
14. Nodier, *Contes,* p. 35.
15. Nodier, *Contes,* p. 330.

16. Nodier, *Contes*, p. 330.
17. Nodier, *Contes*, p. 330.
18. Nodier, *Contes*, p. 331.
19. Nodier, *Contes*, p. 177.
20. Nodier, *Contes*, p. 231.
21. Nodier, *Contes*, p. 144.
22. Nodier, *Contes*, p. 184.
23. Nodier, *Contes*, p. 176.
24. Nodier, *Contes*, p. 390.
25. Nodier, *Contes*, p. 319.
26. Nodier, *Contes*, p. 380.
27. Nodier, *Contes*, p. 232.
28. Nodier, *Contes*, p. 183.
29. Nodier, *Contes*, p. 315.
30. Nodier, *Contes*, p. 180. The mandrake is a forklike root resembling a human torso. The notion that it has magical qualities goes back to antiquity. In Genesis, Leah, the wife of Jacob, received the mandrake, which presumably resulted in the birth of Issachar. In *Song of Songs* mention is made of the perfume of the mandrake. Pliny, in his *Natural History*, gives details and precautions in connection with the mandrake. Machiavelli wrote a play called *The Mandrake*. The Germans such as Novalis, Achim von Arnim, Goethe, and others, made much of the mandrake in their works.
31. Nodier, *Contes*, p. 313.
32. Nodier, *Contes*, p. 185.
33. Vampires are usually adorned with long canine teeth, presumably a sign of man's animal nature as well as sexuality. It is thus rather puzzling to discover that the Fée aux Miettes is provided with teeth similar to those of vampires. Does this imply that the Fée aux Miettes may have latent sexual and animalistic traits?
34. Nodier, *Contes*, p. 297.
35. Nodier, *Contes*, p. 317.
36. Nodier, *Contes*, p. 245.
37. Nodier, *Contes*, p. 240.
38. Nodier, *Contes*, p. 249.
39. Jules Vodoz, *La Fée aux miettes, essai sur le rôle du subconscient dans l'oeuvre de Charles Nodier* (Paris: Champion, 1925), p. 148.
40. Vodoz, p. 250.
41. Vodoz, p. 250.
42. Vodoz, p. 119.
43. Nodier, *Contes*, p. 333.
44. Nodier, *Contes*, p. 334.
45. Nodier, *Contes*, p. 335.

46. Nodier, *Contes*, p. 341.
47. Nodier, *Contes*, p. 341.
48. Nodier, *Contes*, p. 341.
49. Nodier, *Contes*, p. 342.
50. Nodier, *Contes*, p. 343.
51. Nodier, *Contes*, p. 341.
52. Nodier, *Contes*, p. 346.
53. Nodier, *Contes*, p. 347.
54. Nodier, *Contes*, pp. 347–48.
55. Nodier, *Oeuvres complètes*, VIII, 364.
56. Nodier, *Contes*, pp. 71–72.
57. Nodier, *Contes*, p. 71.
58. Nodier, *Contes*, p. 271; *Oeuvres complètes*, IX, 296.
59. Nodier, *Contes*, p. 271.
60. Nodier, *Contes*, p. 271. See also *Souvenirs de la Révolution*.
61. Nodier, *Contes*, p. 351.
62. Nodier, *Contes*, p. 358.
63. Nodier, *Contes*, p. 361.
64. Nodier, *Contes*, p. 367.

### Chapter Six

1. Nodier, *Contes*, p. 390.
2. Nodier is not alone in his attacks on the idea of progress and perfectibility. Gautier in his preface to *Mademoiselle de Maupin* and Baudelaire in *Fusées* and his prose poem entitled *Assommons les pauvres* condemn these notions with equal vigor.
3. Nodier, *Oeuvres complètes*, V, 244.
4. Nodier, *Oeuvres complètes*, V, 251.
5. Nodier, "Qu'est-ce que la Vérité," *Revue de Paris*, XXV (1836), 123.
6. Nodier, *Oeuvres complètes*, V, 305.
7. Nodier, *Oeuvres complètes*, V, 303.
8. Nodier, *Oeuvres complètes*, V, 270.
9. Nodier, *Oeuvres complètes*, V, 285.
10. Nodier, *Contes*, p. 645.
11. Nodier, *Contes*, pp. 645–46.
12. Jean Richer, "Autour de l'Histoire du Roi de Bohême, Charles Nodier 'dériseur sensé,' suivi de La Plus petite des pantoufles par Charles Nodier," *Archives des Lettres Modernes*, 42 (1962), 29.
13. Jean Richer, p. 31.
14. Jean Richer, p. 33.
15. Alfred Jarry, *Selected Works* (New York: Grove Press, 1965), p. 193.
16. Richer, pp. 35–36.

17. Nodier, *Histoire du Roi de Bohême et de ses sept châteaux* (Paris: Delangle Frères, 1830), p. 21.

18. Nodier, *Roi de Bohême*, p. 23.

19. Nodier, *Roi de Bohême*, p. 4.

20. Nodier, *Roi de Bohême*, p. 386.

21. Nodier, *Roi de Bohême*, p. 7.

22. Jean Richer, p. 9.

23. Nodier, *Oeuvres complètes*, V, 54.

24. Nodier, *Contes*, pp. 460–61.

25. Nodier, *Roi de Bohême*, pp. 99–100.

26. Nodier, *Roi de Bohême*, p. 105.

27. Nodier, *Roi de Bohême*, pp. 106–7.

28. Nodier, *Roi de Bohême*, p. 320.

29. Nodier, *Roi de Bohême*, p. 380.

30. Nodier, *Roi de Bohême*, pp. 377–78.

31. Nodier, *Roi de Bohême*, p. 379.

32. Nodier, *Roi de Bohême*, pp. 397–98. A parlor game where each player must respond to the question "Que met-on dans mon corbillon?" (What does one put in my little basket?) by giving a line that rhymes with "on".

33. Nodier, *Roi de Bohême*, p. 205.

34. Nodier, *Oeuvres complètes*, XI, 11.

35. Nodier, *Oeuvres complètes*, XI, 10.

36. Nodier, *Oeuvres complètes*, XI, 4–5.

37. Nodier, *Oeuvres complètes*, XI, 23–24.

38. Nodier, *Contes*, p. 399.

39. Nodier, *Contes*, p. 400.

40. Nodier, *Contes*, p. 449.

41. Nodier, *Contes*, p. 396.

42. Nodier, *Contes*, p. 457.

43. Nodier, *Contes*, p. 458.

44. Nodier, *Contes*, p. 458.

45. Nodier, *Contes*, p. 773.

46. Nodier, *Contes*, p. 774.

## Chapter Seven

1. Nodier's essay on Palingenesis, published in the *Revue de Paris*, brought about a response from Balzac which he published in *Lettre à Charles Nodier sur la palingénésie humaine*. See Nodier, *Contes*, for a discussion by Castex (pp. 843–44).

2. Nodier, *Oeuvres complètes*, V, 343–44.

3. Nodier, *Oeuvres complètes*, V, 384.

4. Nodier, *Oeuvres complètes*, V, 385–86.

5. Nodier, *Contes*, p. 657.

6. Nodier, *Contes,* pp. 782–83.
7. Nodier, *Contes,* p. 789.
8. Nodier, *Contes,* p. 796.
9. Nodier, *Contes,* p. 862.
10. Nodier, *Contes,* p. 864.
11. Nodier, *Contes,* p. 865.
12. Nodier, *Contes,* p. 900.
13. Nodier, *Contes,* p. 899.

## Chapter Eight

1. Schenck, p. 3.
2. Schenck, p. 15.
3. Pingaud, p. 253.
4. Helen Maxwell King, *Les Doctrines littéraires de la Quotidienne, 1814–1830.* Smith College Studies in Modern Languages, Vol. I. (Northhampton, Mass.: Smith College; Paris: Champion, 1919), 50.
5. King, p. 92.
6. King, p. 94.
7. King, p. 95.
8. King, p. 95.
9. King, p. 95.
10. King, p. 96.
11. King, p. 96.
12. King, p. 98.
13. King, p. 78.
14. King, p. 79.
15. King, pp. 99–100.
16. King, p. 101.
17. King, pp. 102–3.
18. King, pp. 46–47.
19. King, p. 104.
20. King, pp. 106–7.
21. King, p. 126.
22. King, p. 154.
23. King, p. 124.
24. King, pp. 157–58.
25. King, p. 159.
26. Victor Hugo, *Three Plays* (New York: Washington Square Press, 1964), pp. 4, 5.
27. Schenck, p. 115.
28. Schenck, p. 116.
29. N. Wilson, "Charles Nodier, Victor Hugo and *Les Feuilles d'Automne,*" *The Modern Language Review,* LX (1965), p. 23.
30. Wilson, p. 23.

31. Nodier, "Les Feuilles d'automne de Victor Hugo," *Revue de Paris*, XXXIII (1831), 114.

32. Nodier, *Feuilles d'automne de Victor Hugo*, p. 116.

33. King, note, p. 50.

34. King, p. 50.

35. King, p. 169.

36. Schenck, p. 19.

37. Schenck, p. 19.

38. Schenck, p. 20.

39. O. G. Brockett, "Charles Nodier's Estimate of Shakespeare," *Shakespeare Quarterly*, XII (1961), 347.

40. Brockett, p. 347.

41. King, p. 102.

42. Nodier, *Oeuvres complètes*, V, 50, 51.

43. Nodier, *Oeuvres complètes*, V, 51.

44. Nodier, *Oeuvres complètes*, V, 49.

45. King, p. 109.

46. Nodier, *Oeuvres complètes*, V, 53.

47. Schenck, p. 23.

48. Schenck, p. 23.

49. One of the legends, dear to many German and French Romanticists, was the legend of the fairy Mélusine or Ondine, half woman, half fish or serpent, who, betrayed by her husband, vanished back into the netherworld, uttering a tragic cry, a cry that André Breton was to hear again during World War II (*Arcane 17*, pp. 91–94).

### Chapter Nine

1. G. Guilleminault, *Les Années folles* (Paris: Denoel, 1956), p. 33.

2. Jacques Vaché, *Lettres de Guerre* (Paris: Eric Losfeld, 1970), p. 61. First appeared as a letter to A. Breton, May 9, 1918. Also quoted in Breton, *Anthologie de l'humour noir* (Paris: Éditions du Sagittaire, 1950), p. 296; and H. Richter, *Dada: Art and Anti-Art* (New York: McGraw-Hill, n.d.), p. 172.

3. André Breton, *Manifestoes of Surrealism* (Ann Arbor: University of Michigan Press, 1969), p. 14. The use of the term "absolute reality" seems to imply a superreality, the Platonic Idea, the archetype, a notion also present in Nerval and Gautier. It is, indeed, true that the Surrealists, like many Romanticists, were Platonic in their attitude toward art; both groups considered the poet to be inspired and irrational, if not mad. Plato's *Ion* could serve as the credo of both groups. "For the poet is a light and winged and holy thing, and there is no invention in him until he has been inspired and is out of his senses, and the mind is no longer in him: when he has not attained to this state, he is powerless and is unable to utter his oracles . . . for not by art does

the poet sing, but by power divine. Had he learned by rules of art, he would have known how to speak not of one theme, but of all; and therefore God takes away the minds of poets, and uses them as his ministers, as he also uses diviners and holy prophets to be speaking not of themselves who utter these priceless words in a state of unconsciousness, but that God himself is the speaker, and that through them he is conversing with us." (*The Dialogues of Plato,* transl. by B. Jowett, I, New York: Random House, 1937, p. 289.)

4. Breton, *Les Pas perdus* (Paris: Gallimard, 1924), p. 149.

5. Nerval, *Oeuvres,* I, 158–59. See also p. 3, same volume and edition, for the poem in question.

6. Nodier, *Contes,* p. 43.

7. Nodier, *Contes,* p. 34.

8. Nodier, *Oeuvres complètes,* IX, 300–1.

# Selected Bibliography

## PRIMARY SOURCES

NODIER, CHARLES. *Oeuvres complètes.* 12 volumes. Geneva: Slatkine Reprints, 1968. Reimpression of the Renduel edition which appeared in Paris between 1832 and 1837. Not complete.

——. *Contes.* Paris: Éditions Garnier Frères, 1961.

——. *Contes fantastiques.* Paris: J.-J. Pauvert, 1957.

——. *Histoire du Roi de Bohême et de ses sept châteaux.* Paris: Slatkine Reprints, 1967.

——. "Les Feuilles d'automne," *Revue de Paris,* 33 (1831), 110–17.

——. "Qu'est-ce que la Vérité?", *Revue de Paris,* 25 (1836), 122–25.

## SECONDARY SOURCES

1. Books

BAYS, GWENDOLYN. *Orphic Vision: Seer Poets from Novalis to Rimbaud.* Lincoln: University of Nebraska Press, 1964. A very good analysis of the occult and Illuminism in the eighteenth and nineteenth centuries. Several pages are devoted to Nodier's innocents.

BÉGUIN, ALBERT. *L'Ame romantique et le rêve.* Paris: José Corti, 1963. A study of the dream in the works of several German Romanticists. A part of the book is devoted to a number of French Romanticists, Nodier included.

BELL, SARAH FORE. *Charles Nodier: His Life and Works.* A Critical Bibliography, 1923–67. Chapel Hill: University of North Carolina Press, 1971. A comprehensive critical bibliography which continues the work of Jean Larat. An invaluable work for the Nodier scholar.

BENDER, EDMUND J. *Bibliographie: Charles Nodier. Bibliographie des oeuvres, des lettres et des manuscrits de Charles Nodier, suivie d'une Bibliographie choisie des études sur Nodier, 1840–1966.* Lafayette, Indiana: Purdue University Studies, 1969. A comprehensive bibliography which includes a catalogue of works, letters, and manuscripts of Nodier.

————. *Charting French Romanticism: The Criticism of Charles Nodier*. Dissertation. Indiana University, 1968. A study of Nodier as literary critic and pioneer of French Romanticism.

CASTEX, PIERRE-GEORGES. *Anthologie du conte fantastique français*. Paris: Corti, 1963. Contains an excerpt from Nodier's *Smarra* and a brief introduction.

————. *Le Conte fantastique en France de Nodier à Maupassant*. Paris: Corti, 1962. A discussion of the *conte fantastique* in general. Nodier is considered an important contributor to the genre.

ESTIGNARD, A. *Correspondance inédite de Charles Nodier*. Paris: Petiau, 1877. An important book containing much of Nodier's correspondence. Difficult to obtain.

HELD, MARIETTE. *Charles Nodier et le romantisme*. Dissertation. Bienne: Editions du Chandelier, 1949. Defines Nodier's role in the Romantic movement, his propensity for the fantastic and the dream, as well as exoticism, the Middle Ages and the influence of German and English literature on his works.

JUIN, HUBERT. *Charles Nodier*. Paris: Éditions Pierre Seghers, 1970. A study of Nodier's life and times. Little discussion of his works.

KELLER, LUZIUS. *Piranèse et les romantiques*. Paris: Corti, 1966. An analysis of the impact of the art of Piranesi on Nodier, Nerval, Gautier, Baudelaire, and others via De Quincey.

KING, HELEN MAXWELL. *Les Doctrines littéraires de la Quotidienne, 1814–1830*. Smith College Studies in Modern Languages, Vol. I. Northhampton, Mass.: Smith College; Paris: Champion, 1919. A study of the monarchist newspaper *La Quotidienne*, its attitude toward Romanticism and its relationship to Nodier, Hugo, and others.

LARAT, JEAN. *Bibliographie critique des oeuvres de Charles Nodier, suivie de documents inédits*. Bibliothèque de la Revue de Littérature Comparée, Vol. X. Paris: Champion, 1923. A comprehensive bibliography covering the period up to 1923.

————. *La Tradition de l'exotisme dans l'oeuvre de Charles Nodier (1780–1844). Étude sur les origines du romantisme français*. Bibliothèque de la Revue de Littérature Comparée, Vol. IX. Paris: Champion, 1923. This study concerns itself primarily with the successive influences and themes in the works of Nodier, such as exoticism and the revival of a national tradition.

MAIXNER, RUDOLF. *Charles Nodier et l'Illyrie*. Paris: Didier, 1960. A study of Nodier's sojourn and interest in Illyria, its history, literature, folklore, and language.

MENESSIER-NODIER, MARIE. *Charles Nodier, Épisodes et souvenirs de sa vie*. Paris: Didier, 1867. A very personal account of some episodes in the life of Nodier recounted by his daughter.

MILNER, MAX. *Le Diable dans la littérature française de Cazotte à Baudelaire*. 2 vols. Paris: Corti, 1960. A discussion of the frenetic and Satanism in French literature, which includes Nodier's own contributions to the field.

OLIVER, A. RICHARD. *Charles Nodier, Pilot of Romanticism*. Syracuse, N.Y.: Syracuse University Press, 1964. Primarily devoted to the life and times of Nodier, his contributions to the development of Romanticism, his relationship to Victor Hugo. Little literary criticism.

PINGAUD, LÉONCE. *La Jeunesse de Charles Nodier*. Besançon: Dodivers, 1914, Discussion of Nodier as an early proponent of Romanticism. Important early letters are also included.

SALOMON, MICHEL. *Charles Nodier et le groupe romantique*. Paris: Perrin, 1908. A study of Nodier and other Romanticists in the context of the times.

SCHENCK, EUNICE MORGAN. *La Part de Charles Nodier dans la formation des idées romantiques de Victor Hugo jusqu'à la préface de Cromwell*. Paris: Champion, 1914. Nodier's contributions to Romanticism before the *Préface de Cromwell* are discussed.

SCHNEIDER, MARCEL. *La Littérature fantastique en France*. Paris: Fayard, 1964. A detailed study of the fantastic in French literature as well as the influence of such men as Hoffmann, Poe, and the gothic novel. Nodier's *La Fée aux miettes* is discussed in terms of the fantastic and its link with Hoffmann.

VIATTE, AUGUSTE. *Les Sources occultes du romantisme: illuminisme-théosophie, 1770–1820*. Paris: Champion, 1965. A detailed scholarly study of the occult and illuminism in the 18th and 19th centuries and their influence on several Romanticists, Nodier included.

VODOZ, JULES. *"La Fée aux miettes." Essai sur le rôle du subconscient dans l'oeuvre de Charles Nodier*. Paris: Champion, 1925. A psychoanalytical study of Nodier's *La Fée aux miettes*. An attempt to penetrate the deep recesses of Nodier's mind via this work.

2. Articles

ASSELINEAU, CHARLES. "Nouvelle étude sur Charles Nodier." *Bulletin du Bibliophile*. Paris, 1867. Sees Nodier as an important contributor to the new movement. Valuable as a testimony of one who was part of the movement.

BÉGUIN, ALBERT. "Charles Nodier ou l'enfance restaurée." *Cahiers du*

*Sud,* 304 (1950), 353–57. Explains *Trilby* and *La Fée aux miettes* in terms of Nodier's desire for a primordial paradise. Also discusses Vodoz' psychoanalytical study of this work.

————. "Nodier et Nerval." *Labyrinthe,* 1 (October 15, 1944), 7. An analysis of Nodier's influence on Nerval's works, especially with respect to portraits of young girls in *Sylvie* and *Thérèse Aubert.*

BROCKETT, O. G. "Charles Nodier's Estimate of Shakespeare," *Shakespeare Quarterly,* 12 (1961), 345–48. An analysis of Nodier as an admirer of Shakespeare primarily for his moral teachings, supports the idea that Nodier is no different from other Frenchmen of his time.

CASTEX, PIERRE-GEORGES. "Balzac et Charles Nodier," in *L'Année balzacienne,* 1962. Paris: Garnier Frères, 1962. A discussion of the reciprocal borrowings and influences between Nodier and Balzac in the early 1930's.

————. "Une Source de la Fée aux Miettes," *Revue des Sciences Humaines,* n.s., 1950, pp. [205]–8. An attempt to explain why Nodier placed the lunatic asylum in *La Fée aux miettes* in Glasgow.

CHARLES, PAUL-A. "Charles Nodier et Victor Hugo." *Revue d'Histoire Littéraire de la France,* 39 (1932), 568–86. A discussion of Nodier's relationship to Hugo with respect to *Marion Delorme.*

DECOTTIGNIES, JEAN. "Variations sur un succube: *Histoire de Thibaud de la Jacquière," Revue des Sciences Humaines,* n.s., 111 (1963), [329]–40. A discussion of the source of Nodier's tale in Jean Potocki's work of 1914.

DEHARME, LISE. "Charles Nodier," in Francis Dumont, ed., *Les Petits Romantiques français.* Ligugé: Les Cahiers du Sud, 1949. Creative rather than scholarly, denoting an aesthetic appreciation of Nodier's work.

FONGARO, ANTOINE. "A-t-on lu la Fée aux Miettes?" *Revue des Sciences,* n.s., 107 (1962), [439]–52. To the psychoanalytical approach of Vodoz and the ethical and moral approach of Lebois, Fongaro puts forth his own interpretation: a gnostic and Catharist explanation of the work.

LEBOIS, ANDRÉ. "Un Bréviaire du compagnonnage: *La Fée aux Miettes* de Charles Nodier." *Archives des Lettres Modernes,* 40 (1961), 40 pp. *La Fée aux miettes* is seen as a moral tale for adult education, expressing the basic ideas of Freemasonry.

MENESSIER-NODIER, JEAN. "Charles Nodier et l'éducation du peuple, pages inédites," *Revue des Sciences Humaines,* n.s., 76 (1954), [393]–401. Nodier is discussed here not merely as one who opposed collective education, but as one who was also interested in technical and moral education in a more positive way.

OLIVER, A. RICHARD. "Charles Nodier and the Marquis de Sade."

*Modern Language Notes,* 75 (1960), 497–502. An attempt to show that Nodier never met Sade as he claims to have done.

———. "Charles Nodier's Cult of Shakespeare as a Facet of French Romanticism," *Orbis Litterarum, Revue Internationale d'Études Littéraires,* 17 (1962), 154–65. A discussion of Nodier as an admirer of Shakespeare and his use of Shakespeare to introduce Romanticism into France.

———. "Nodier as Bibliographer and Bibliophile," *Library Quarterly,* 26 (1956), 23–30. Discusses Nodier's place as one of the great bibliophiles of all times and his publication of the *Bulletin du Bibliophile.*

POULET, GEORGES. "Piranèse et les poètes romantiques," in his *Trois Essais de mythologie romantique.* Paris: Corti, 1966. A study of Piranesi's staircase on 19th century French writers.

RICHER, JEAN. "Autour de *L'Histoire du roi de Bohême,* Charles Nodier 'dériseur sensé', suivi de *La plus petite des pantoufles* par Charles Nodier," *Archives des Lettres Modernes,* 42 (1962). Paris: Lettres Modernes, 1962. A composite of several articles on Nodier, letters, and an unpublished tale.

———. "Nodier et Nerval," *Cahiers du Sud,* 304 (1950), 364–71. The influence of Nodier on Nerval with respect to their portraits of young girls.

RUFF, MARCEL. "Maturin et les romantiques français," in C. R. Maturin *Bertram, ou le château de Saint-Aldobrand.* Traduit librement de l'anglais par Taylor et Ch. Nodier. Éd. commentée et précédée d'une introduction sur Maturin et le romantiques français par Marcel A. Ruff.

SAINTE-BEUVE, CHARLES-AUGUSTIN. "Charles Nodier," *Revue des deux mondes,* 2 (1840), 377–409. A favorable portrait of Nodier by a contemporary.

SWITZER, RICHARD. "Charles Nodier: A Re-examination," *The French Review,* 28 (1954–55), 224–32. A reconsideration of Nodier as an early exponent of Romanticism and a precursor of Symbolism, especially evident in his *Smarra* and *Le Roi de Bohême.*

WILSON, N. "Charles Nodier, Victor Hugo and *Les Feuilles d'automne,*" *The Modern Language Review,* 60 (1965), 21–31. An attempt to explain the composition of Hugo's *Feuilles d'automne* in terms of Nodier's relationship to Hugo.

# Index

(The works of Charles Nodier are listed under his name)

*183*